# The Blue Riband of the Heather

## THE SUPREME CHAMPIONS
## 1906–95

*J. M. Wilson with (left) Whitehope Nap 8685 and (right) Bill 9040*

# The Blue Riband of the Heather

## THE SUPREME CHAMPIONS
## 1906–95

# E. B. Carpenter

*Farming Press*

*First published 1989*
*Second edition 1996*

Copyright © E. B. Carpenter 1989 & 1996

ISBN 0 852 36 318 4

A catalogue record for this book
is available from the British Library

**Published by Farming Press Books**
**Miller Freeman Professional Ltd**
**Wharfedale Road, Ipswich IP1 4LG, United Kingdom**

Distributed in North America
by Diamond Farm Enterprises,
Box 537, Alexandria Bay, NY 13607, USA

Typeset by Galleon Typesetting, Ipswich
Printed and bound in Great Britain by Butler & Tanner, Frome, Somerset

# Contents

## FIGURES

*This book I dedicate to the memory of my husband, Will,
and to my dear friends Sheila Grew and Barbara Houseman,
who all enjoyed and appreciated the companionship
of their Border Collies.*

# Preface

THIS collection of photographs has been put together as a tribute to the Border Collie, so successfully bred to do the work for which it has been developed, wherever sheep are shepherded, and in gratitude to my own Border Collies, my companions in work and leisure, through whom I have gained many, many treasured friends.

I am so very grateful to all who have supplied the photographs, for without their generosity in lending treasured pictures this book would not have been possible. I thank the photographers for permission to use their photographs, and apologise to those whom I cannot trace. My special thanks to Mr G. Caldwell who has so ably reproduced these photographs, many from old agricultural papers, etc., and to my sister, Ruth Hirst, for typing copy and proofreading. Thanks also to the sculptor and sheepdog handler Austin Bennett for several photographs and especially for the drawings of Don 17 and Sweep 21.

If the only available picture of a dog was poor, I have nevertheless included it as part of the record. Perhaps for the next edition, readers will be able to supply better ones.

The data have been taken from the International Sheep Dog Society stud books, trials programmes, trophy award books, etc. The numbers displayed after the dogs' names are their stud book registra-tion numbers. I am also grateful to the International Sheep Dog Society for permission to reproduce material from its literature, especially in the opening section on development of the Society's trials.

A few lines have been written about some of the most successful families of International Sheep Dog Society competition fame, for the handling of sheep and dogs seems to be 'bred' in these families as deeply as the working instinct is in the Border Collie.

Much can be learned of the history and romance of the breed from Eric Halsall's *Sheepdogs, My Faithful Friends* and *Sheepdog Trials*, and Sheila Grew's two volumes of *Key Dogs*, books that give a fascinating, comprehensive history of a century of clever stockmanship.

Interesting information too can be gained from reading Peidje Vidler's *The Border Collie in Australasia* for she has thoroughly researched into the Australian and New Zealand lines that stem from British exports in the early part of this century.

I wish to thank Eric Halsall for his Foreword.

*E. B. Carpenter*
*Pastors Hill House*
*Bream, 1989*

## Note to the Second Edition

For additional interest I have included the third generation in the pedigrees of these Supreme Champions and have updated these awards to 1995. Any previous omissions in the awards have been rectified.

# Foreword

THESE are the élite. These are the wisest of the wisest dogs in the world. These collie dogs which are portrayed and detailed with their achievements in this book are truly the super-stars of the canine world. Barbara Carpenter has done a good job in collecting them all together under one roof – between the covers of this book – and in doing so, she has not only given us who know and respect the working sheepdog a concise and authoritive reference to the cream of canine aristocracy, compiled a book which will bring pleasure to everyone who appreciates dogs, but, perhaps of even greater importance, she has filled a niche for the agricultural historian.

Without these dogs, and their contemporaries, the sheep flocks of the world could not be managed. We who spend our lives with them know their value to the agricultural economy of the world.

We talk glibly and often in awe of Scott's Kep, Brown's Spot, Roberts's Jaff, and the like, but few of us actually saw them in action, so it is good to see them if only in pictorial form, and the information which goes along with the pictures puts every dog into perspective.

Breeding counts – everyone involved with livestock knows this to be true. Britain, for long the stud-farm of the world on all counts, can no longer make this claim – except in one aspect. British collies are still the best in the world, and the world still draws its collie strength from Britain. This book, intelligently read, shows why this is so.

Only one collie wins a Supreme Championship each year, and it is usually a great dog, for after three trials the luck which goes with all contests is reduced to a minimum. A sheepdog's value is tested daily on the sheepruns of Britain, but the Supreme Championship is really the only sound competitive test of a dog's ability.

The dogs which Barbara has listed in these pages could really shepherd sheep. If we study their forebears – and their offspring – we will improve dogs to shepherd the mountain – not just to chase three sheep round a field to win a cup! Dogs which are capable of winning the Supreme Championship are invariably dogs which can be used to improve the breed for its prime purpose of shepherding the sheep runs of the world.

Many of us have written recent books about the modern collie, but this book, researched to such a fine extent by Barbara Carpenter to make a valuable account of wise breeding, beats the lot, for it records that which has gone before, and there is no future without a past.

This book is invaluable on two counts – to the man who breeds sheepdogs to manage his flock to earn a living, and to the agricultural historian.

*Eric Halsall*
*Cliviger, 1989*

# The Blue Riband of the Heather

## THE SUPREME CHAMPIONS
## 1906–95

# The Development of
# the International Sheep Dog Society's Trials

## 1906–14

'The International Sheep Dog Society was formed at Haddington in 1906 by some Scottish sheepdog enthusiasts. In the pre-war period of its existence the Society, though International in name, was mainly Scottish. Its office-bearers and members were chiefly Scotsmen, and of the trials which the Society held annually for nine years before 1914, seven were held in various places in Scotland and two in the North of England. Though the fee was trifling (2/6) the membership in pre-war years never exceeded 100 shepherds and farmers, and, though important from a pastoral point of view, the Society's trials never attracted the public in large numbers. In common with similar societies throughout the country, the Society ceased its activities in the summer of 1914.'

## 1915–21

'The war over, in its military aspect at least, an impersonal something calling itself the Society resumed its work in 1919 with no members, no office-bearers, and a credit balance of £5 from 1914. But members were soon got in sufficient numbers to enable the Society to function once more constitutionally, and since then its work has prospered and developed out of all recognition.
'Two outstanding changes marked post-war beginnings. A stud book was founded.' This 'stimulated wider and deeper interest in the study of pedigree amongst sheep dog men everywhere, there can be no doubt. Next, the Society's trials were reformed.

'In pre-war days the annual trial was only a one-day affair attracting on an average some 15 to 20 farmers and shepherds in Scotland and England with 30 to 40 dogs. All competed in common, there being no "class" distinction between hired shepherds and farmers. The prize money was never large – a cup and some £40 altogether – but the indirect gains by successful competitors at the trials were always such as to attract the best breeders and trainers in the two countries. In particular, the demand for good sheep dogs abroad, especially in Australia and New Zealand, was always sufficiently strong to induce them to compete.

'When the Society resumed its work after the war (1919) two important changes were at once made; hired shepherds and farmers were separated into two classes, and the trial became a two-day affair. . . . By giving them a separate class, interest in the Society's trials among hired shepherds everywhere was immensely stimulated, for they now felt that they could compete with one another on even terms, and that financial gain would reward the successful amongst them as amongst the farmers. . . . This state of matters continued for the three years 1919–21. During these years the Society's influence increased rapidly, so much so that in the autumn of 1921, Wales now invited its attention. In September of that year the Criccieth Sheep Dog Society decided

1

to send its Secretary, Captain Whittaker, Port Madoc, as a deputation to invite the Society to Wales.' He 'attended the Society's trials at Ayr, and as a result of the appeal he made, supported by the Hon. E. L. Mostyn, North Wales (now Lord Mostyn) who was also at the trials as a spectator, and by Mr Jones-Jarrett of Corwen, who was acting as a judge, the Directors unanimously decided to visit Criccieth in 1922.'

## 1922–35

'The trial hitherto being only International in the sense that a dozen or so Scotsmen and two or three Englishmen, chiefly from Yorkshire and Northumberland, took part in it, it was felt that, as Wales had now come within the scope of the Society's operations, something much more definite was required to give the

*Petsoe Queen with her trainer, G. P. Wilkinson, Louth, Lincolnshire*

*Kellys from the Isle of Man*

Society a truly International status. It was therefore decided that each country should have what was called a "National" trial at which a team of dogs could be selected to represent it at an International proper. So the "team" system commenced in 1922 when three National trials were held in Scotland, Wales and England at which teams of 12 dogs were selected to represent each country at the International at Criccieth in September. . . . The final event – the International proper – being now a three days' affair held alternately in each of the three countries.

'These points, in particular, differentiate the Society's trials from all other trials; (1) the trial is not a local affair; in its preliminary stages in each country it is national, and in its final stages International, and (2) the process of elimination is ever at work.'

However, there was a departure from the usual competition in 1927, at the English National at Lancaster, when a class for the Old English Sheep Dog was included, after pressure from the enthusiasts of that breed. Unfortunately, of the six entries (after a promise of 13) for this class, only one was forward, a dark grey bitch, Dr A. L. Tireman's Petsoe Queen.

After the luncheon interval she was put through an exhibition course, having to fetch four sheep from 300 yards and pen them. Apparently, having trotted over for a friendly greeting to the judges, she ambled up the course; the sheep fortunately came down through the fetch gates, but then she refused to give any assistance at the pen, leaving her handler to pen the sheep himself eventually, to the great amusement of the spectators, while she watched from a distance!

No further classes for the Old English Sheep Dog were included in the Society's trials, but at the Scottish National the same year, five competitors from the Isle of Man competed in a class for Irish and Manx dogs.

'Such, briefly, is the history of the development of the Society's trials.'*

* *Quoted extracts are reprinted by permission of the International Sheep Dog Society from their booklet* Blue Riband of the Heather.

3

# Since 1936

This system continued until 1961 when Northern Ireland held a National trial and three dogs went forward to the International qualifying trials. In 1965 the Republic or Eire and Northern Ireland amalgamated to hold the Irish National, four competitors then taking part in the qualifying trial and thus giving a total of 40 dogs from the four countries.

The centenary of trials was celebrated in 1973 at Bala, close to the original trial ground of 1873. In this same year a Society badge was produced with the charismatic Wiston Cap in the design, and the Blue Riband for the Supreme Champion was reintroduced. It is of material, with a clasp to fasten it around the dog's neck.

The year 1976 saw the end of the separate Shepherds' Class, which was combined once again as shepherds and farmers, the championship trophies being awarded to the highest pointed shepherd's dog and the highest pointed farmer's dog in the qualifying trial. At present 15 dogs from England, Scotland and Wales and 10 from Ireland compete in the qualifying trial, with 15 of the highest pointed dogs, irrespective of country, going forward to the Supreme Championship.

These rules continue, the number of National entries being limited by qualification on points, won at affiliated Open trials. A total of 150 singles competitors, plus the brace classes, is considered sufficient for the three-day Nationals. The four-day trials of 1979, 1980 and 1981 were found, for many reasons, not to be practical.

*The first sheepdog trial trophy in the world, won by James Thomson at Rhiwlas, Wales in 1876. Presented to the International Sheep Dog Society by his widow, Jean Thomson, on her 102nd birthday on 1 June 1954*

The current secretary of the ISDS is Mr A. Philip Hendry CBE, The International Sheep Dog Society, Chesham House, 47 Bromham Road, Bedford MK40 2AA.

## Some National Trophies

Alexander Andrew Trophy — Scottish National, highest-pointed Scottish-bred dog or bitch
John H. Thorp Memorial Trophy — English National, highest-pointed English-bred dog or bitch

Challis Shield — Welsh National, highest-pointed Welsh-bred dog or bitch
Ivy Parry Trophy — English National, dog or bitch gaining highest points in outrun, lift and fetch
Warnock Trophy — Scottish National, highest-pointed dog or bitch on first day
Royal Dublin Society Trophy — Irish National, highest-pointed Irish-bred dog or bitch
J.M. Wilson Challenge Shield — Scottish National Championship Winner

# International Trophies 1995

The 1995 awards are listed below. Note that awards made by commercial sponsors can vary from year to year.

The Sun Alliance Shepherds Trophy
The Duchess of Devonshire Farmers' Trophy
The Stirling Team Shield
Subaru Ltd Plate
The C.E.H. Yates English Shepherds' Aggregate Cup
The Lord Mostyn Scottish Shepherds' Aggregate Cup
The J.E. Roebuck Welsh Shepherds' Aggregate Cup
The Omagh Marts Irish Shepherds' Aggregate Cup
The Wilsons Rose Bowl (Brace Champion)
The David Stone Brace Aggregate Cup
The Supreme Championship Third Championship Shield
The Capt. Whittaker Rosebowl (Highest Outwork Points)
The Lord Mostyn Plate (Supreme Champion)
The R. Fortune Trophy (Supreme Champion)
The Ernest Broadley Cup (Breeder of Winner)
The Roberthill Trophy (Sire of Winner)
The Gwilliam Goblet (Breeder of Winner)
Feedmobile Challenge Cup (Runner-up to Supreme Champion)
The McDiarmid Trophy (Bred/handled by Competitor)
The Clara Roebuck Cup (Highest Aggregate Overall, National plus International)
The W.R. Seward English Aggregate Trophy (National plus International)
The J.S. Gray Scottish Aggregate Trophy (National plus International)
The C.D. Fenwick Welsh Aggregate Trophy (National plus International)
The Pennefather Irish Aggregate Trophy (National plus International)
The Edinburgh Trophy (Oldest Competitor)
The Donaldson Cup (Youngest Competitor)
The J.B. Bagshaw Trophy (Driving Champion)
The Ashton Priestley Silver Salver (Best Sportsman)
The Society's Blue Riband (Supreme Champion's Collar)
The Rhiwlas Trophy (Socicty's Oldest Trophy — Supreme Champion)

*Specials*

Pedigree Chum Supreme Championship Trophy
Pedigree Chum Silver Salver (winner of qualifying trial)
Welsh Water Trophy (highest-pointed Welshman)

# Course for National Championships and International Qualifying Trials

(1) *Course* – The Course, Scale of Points and Time Limit now fixed by the Directors are set out below and the responsibility for laying out the Course in accordance with the Rules rests with the Trials Committee and the Course Director.

(2) *Gathering 400 yards* – In the outrun the dog may be directed on either side. A straight fetch from the lift to the handler, through a centre gate (7 yards wide) 150 yards from the handler. No re-try at the gate is allowed. The handler will remain at the post from the commencement of the outrun and at the end of the fetch he will pass the sheep behind him.

(3) *Driving* – The handler will stand at the post and direct his dog to drive the sheep 450 yards over a triangular course through two sets of gates 7 yards wide, a second attempt at either gate is NOT allowed. The drive ends when the sheep enter the shedding ring. The handler will remain at the post until the sheep are in the shedding ring. In the case of a short course, when the fetch is less than 400 yards, the drive will be lengthened when possible so that the total length of the fetch and drive is 850 yards, or as near to the length as is reasonably practicable. The drive may be either to left or right and shall be decided by the Trials Committee immediately prior to the Trial.

(4) *Shedding* – Two unmarked sheep to be shed within a ring 40 yards in diameter. The dog must be in full control of the two sheep shed (in or outside the ring) otherwise the shed will not be deemed satisfactory. On completion of the shed the handler shall reunite his sheep before proceeding to pen.

(5) *Penning* – The pen will be 8 feet by 9 feet with a gate 8 feet wide to which is secured a rope 6 feet long. On completion of shedding, the handler must proceed to the pen, leaving his dog to bring the sheep to the pen. The handler is forbidden to assist the dog to drive the sheep to the pen. The handler will stand at the gate holding the rope and must not let go of the rope while the dog works the sheep into the pen. The handler will close the gate. After releasing the sheep, the handler will close and fasten the gate.

(6) *Single sheep* – The handler will proceed to the shedding ring leaving the dog to bring the sheep from the pen to the ring. One of two marked sheep will be shed off within the ring and thereafter worn (in or outside the ring) to the judges' satisfaction. Handlers are forbidden to assist the dog in driving off, or attempting to drive off the single any distance or by forcing it on the dog.

5 SHEEP

GATHER

400 YARDS FETCH

DRIVE 150 YARDS

SHEDDING RING

DRIVE 150 YDS

PEN
8 ft BY 9 ft

SHEDDING RING
40 YDS DIAMETER
IN FRONT OF SHEPHERD

SINGLE SHEEP IN
SHEDDING RING

**SCALE OF POINTS** – Outrun 20; Lifting 10; Fetching 20; Driving 30; Shedding 10; Penning 10; Single 10. **Total 110** per Judge (Aggregate 440)

**TIME LIMIT** – 15 minutes. No extension.

# Course for International Brace Championship

*Course –*

(1) *Gathering* – There will be 10 or such number of sheep as the Committee decide upon, in one lot in the centre of the field at a distance of approximately 800 yards. Both dogs will start at the same time. Crossing at the completion of the outrun is permissible but dogs should remain on the side to which they have crossed and they should not recross. The fetch should be straight through a gate (9 yards wide) in the centre of the field. Should the gate be missed no re-try is allowed. Each dog will keep to its own side and the handler will remain at the post and at the end of the fetch will pass the sheep behind him.

(2) *Driving* – The handler stands at the post and directs his two dogs to drive the sheep 600 yards over a triangular course through two sets of gates (9 yards wide), back to the handler. No re-try is allowed at either gate. Each dog is to keep to its own side and handler must remain at the post until the end of the drive. The drive is finished when the sheep enter the shedding ring.

(3) *Shedding* – The sheep will be divided into two equal lots by either dog inside the shedding ring; one lot will be driven off and left in charge of one dog – the other lot will be penned in a diamond shaped pen with an entrance of 5 feet and no gate. This dog will be left in charge while the other lot are penned by the other dog in similar pen approximately 50 yards away.

**SCALE OF POINTS** – Gathering 80 (Outrun 2 × 20 = 40; Lifting 20 and Fetching 20); Driving 30; Shedding 10; Penning (2 × 10) 20. **Total 140** per Judge (Aggregate 560).
**TIME LIMIT** – 25 minutes. No extension.

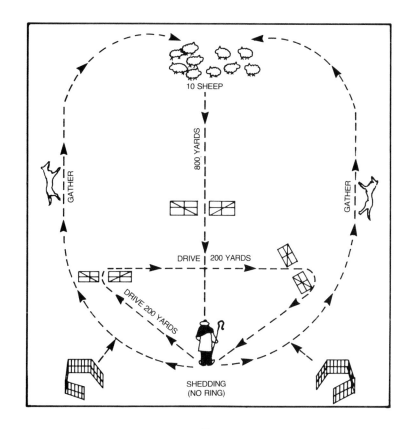

# Course for International Supreme Championship

## (Restricted to 15 highest pointed dogs in Qualifying Trials irrespective of Country or Class)

**SCALE OF POINTS** – Gathering 100 (each Outrun 20; each Lift 10; each Fetch 20); Driving 40; Shedding 20; Penning 10. **Total 170.**
**TIME LIMIT** – 30 minutes. No extension.

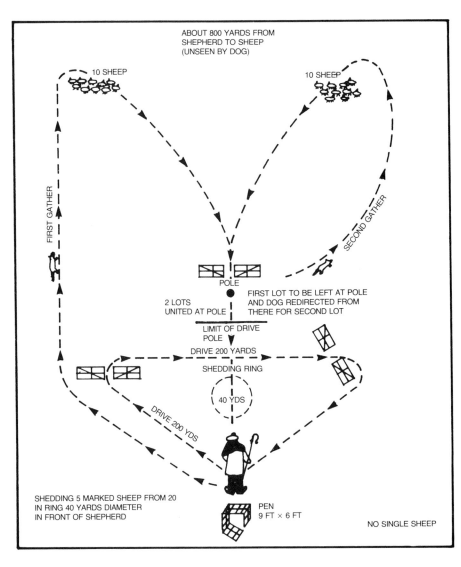

ABOUT 800 YARDS FROM
SHEPHERD TO SHEEP
(UNSEEN BY DOG)

10 SHEEP

10 SHEEP

FIRST GATHER

SECOND GATHER

POLE

FIRST LOT TO BE LEFT AT POLE
AND DOG REDIRECTED FROM
THERE FOR SECOND LOT

2 LOTS
UNITED AT POLE

LIMIT OF DRIVE
POLE

DRIVE 200 YARDS

SHEDDING RING

40 YDS

DRIVE 200 YDS

SHEDDING 5 MARKED SHEEP FROM 20
IN RING 40 YARDS DIAMETER
IN FRONT OF SHEPHERD

PEN
9 FT × 6 FT

NO SINGLE SHEEP

*COURSE –*

*(1) Gathering –* Distance about 800 yards for one lot of 10 sheep (if possible unseen by the dog) which should be brought through the gate (9 yards wide) in the centre of the field to a post fixed 20 yards through the gate; the dog having reached the post will then be re-directed for another lot of sheep (if possible unseen by the dog) which should also be brought through the gate and united with the first lot. The first run to be right or left as decided by the Trials Committee before the Trial and all competitors will run on that side, the second run to be on the other side. Should the gate be missed no re-try is allowed. Both the dog and the first lot of sheep must be past the gate to the post 20 yards inside the gate before the dog is re-directed for the second lot. At the end of the fetch the handler shall pass the sheep behind him.

(2) *Driving –* The drive shall be for 600 yards from where the handler stands in a triangular course through two gate obstacles (9 yards wide), back to the handler. The drive may be right or left as directed. Should the gates be missed no re-try is permitted at either gate. The drive should be in straight lines and ends when the sheep enter the shedding ring. The handler will remain at the post until the drive is finished.

(3) *Shedding –* The fifteen unmarked sheep to be shed off within a ring 40 yards in diameter. In shedding the sheep will be passed between the handler and his dog and the dog brought in to stop and turn back the marked sheep. Manoeuvring for 'cuts' is not allowed. Should any marked sheep leave the shedding ring and join any unmarked sheep already shed off the unmarked sheep with which the marked sheep has joined will be brought into the ring and shedding re-started. Until the fifteen unmarked sheep are shed off penning will not be permitted.

(4) *Penning –* The five marked sheep must be penned and the gate shut. The pen will be 8 feet by 9 feet with a gate 8 feet wide, to which is secured a rope 6 feet long. On completion of shedding, the handler must proceed to the pen, leaving the dog to bring the sheep to the pen. The handler is forbidden to assist his dog in driving the sheep to the pen. The handler will stand at the gate holding the rope and must not let go of the rope, while the dog works the sheep into the pen. The handler must close the gate. After releasing the sheep, the handler will close and fasten the gate.

(5) *General –* No points will be awarded for work done in the shedding ring or at the pen when either of these phases of the work has not been completed within the prescribed time limit.

# OLD HEMP

OLD HEMP was born September 1893 and died May 1901. He was bred by Adam Telfer from the good-natured, plain working, black and tan Roy, out of the strong-eyed, shy, black-coated Meg, who were both from a line of sound old Northumberland-bred collies. Hemp was a 'natural', handling sheep with the true, easy power of the quality sheepdog – the power and method that sheep respond to with respect and confidence. Sheep men were impressed by Hemp's qualities and used him on their bitches. Such was his prepotency that the majority of his puppies worked with similar quiet method, and the strain became popular and established, shepherds realising that dogs working with Hemp's style and method caused less stress to their flocks.

Sheepdog trials, particularly those of the International Sheep Dog Society, are the means whereby the standards of the dogs' prowess and stamina are assessed. Their performances show the degree of success of past and present breeding policies, and influence those of the future.

The success of these Supreme Champions must in no small way depend on the clever blending of the various lines within the 'family' of registered dogs, all stemming from the same root stock – Adam Telfer's Hemp 9 and J. Scott's Kep 13, who, though not in direct line to Hemp, was from Cleg, a granddaughter of Hemp's grandam, Pose. Kep's misalliance with his own dam, Cleg, resulted in a family line blending well with the main Hemp line, and Kep, having a similar quiet, firm method of work, became almost as popular a stud dog as Hemp.

The family names of the Border flock masters of this time are as famous as their dogs: Thomas Armstrong; the Brown brothers,

*R. D. Sandilands of Queensferry, whose
Supreme Champion Don (see 1906) was
in the line from Cleg*

Andrew, George and Thomas; T. Dickson; George and Tom Gilholm; T. Hunter; J. Scott; A. Telfer; Wm. Wallace, Otterburn and Wm. Wallace, Fingland, to name but a few. All these men, with canny stockmanship, blended these closely related collies to form a sound foundation on which has been built the continuing integrity of the modern Border Collie.

Adam Telfer and his sons Adam and Walter were renowned for their breeding and training of sheepdogs, and soon the fame of Hemp's firm, stylish work spread beyond the local sheep walks, and as his offspring continued to show the great qualities of their sire, his prepotency was fortunately recognised, and he became a popular stud dog.

Three distinct 'family' lines can be traced from Tommy 16, bred by Wm. Wallace, Otterburn. Tommy (a grandson of Hemp) bred to Ancrum Jed, a daughter of Kep, out of Cleg, produced Tyne 145, Moss 22 and Trim 37, each being the direct forbear of a specific line of different Supreme Champions. Bred to A. Brown's Old Maid 1, Tommy produced another line of champions, and bred to G. Brown's Nell 205, yet another distinct line.

Another grandson of Hemp, T. Armstrong's Sweep 21, son of Trim 37, headed the other

*(text continues on page 14)*

*T. Dickson's Hemp 153*

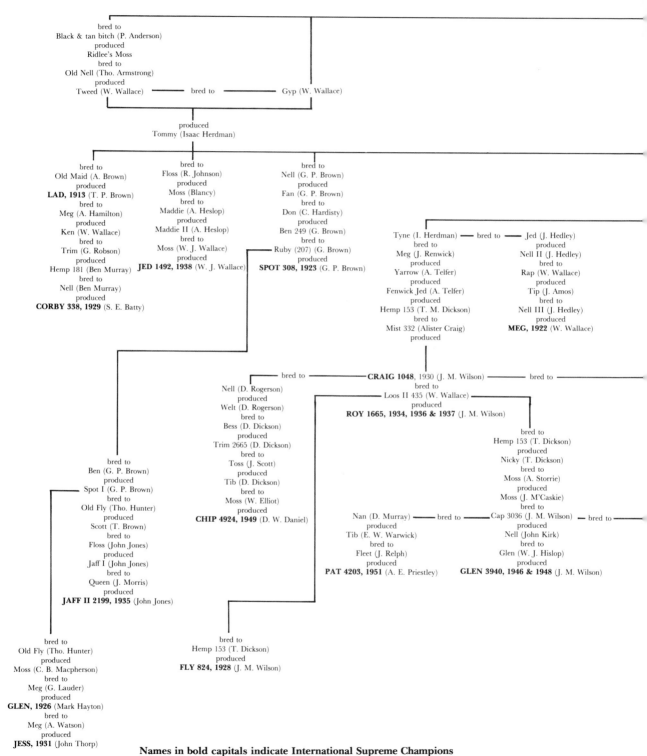

bred to
Black & tan bitch (P. Anderson)
produced
Ridlee's Moss
bred to
Old Nell (Tho. Armstrong)
produced
Tweed (W. Wallace) ——— bred to ——— Gyp (W. Wallace)

produced
Tommy (Isaac Herdman)

bred to
Old Maid (A. Brown)
produced
**LAD, 1913** (T. P. Brown)
bred to
Meg (A. Hamilton)
produced
Ken (W. Wallace)
bred to
Trim (G. Robson)
produced
Hemp 181 (Ben Murray)
bred to
Nell (Ben Murray)
produced
**CORBY 338, 1929** (S. E. Batty)

bred to
Floss (R. Johnson)
produced
Moss (Blancy)
bred to
Maddie (A. Heslop)
produced
Maddie II (A. Heslop)
bred to
Moss (W. J. Wallace)
**JED 1492, 1938** (W. J. Wallace)

bred to
Nell (G. P. Brown)
produced
Fan (G. P. Brown)
bred to
Don (C. Hardisty)
produced
Ben 249 (G. Brown)
bred to
Ruby (207) (G. Brown)
**SPOT 308, 1923** (G. P. Brown)

Tyne (I. Herdman) ——— bred to ——— Jed (J. Hedley)
bred to
Meg (J. Renwick)
produced
Yarrow (A. Telfer)
produced
Fenwick Jed (A. Telfer)
produced
Hemp 153 (T. M. Dickson)
bred to
Mist 332 (Alister Craig)
produced

produced
Nell II (J. Hedley)
bred to
Rap (W. Wallace)
produced
Tip (J. Amos)
bred to
Nell III (J. Hedley)
produced
**MEG, 1922** (W. Wallace)

bred to ——— **CRAIG 1048**, 1930 (J. M. Wilson) ——— bred to
Nell (D. Rogerson)
produced
Welt (D. Rogerson)
bred to
Bess (D. Dickson)
produced
Trim 2665 (D. Dickson)
bred to
Toss (J. Scott)
produced
Tib (D. Dickson)
bred to
Moss (W. Elliot)
produced
**CHIP 4924, 1949** (D. W. Daniel)

bred to
Loos II 435 (W. Wallace)
produced
**ROY 1665, 1934, 1936 & 1937** (J. M. Wilson)

bred to
Hemp 153 (T. Dickson)
produced
Nicky (T. Dickson)
bred to
Moss (A. Storrie)
produced
Moss (J. M'Caskie)
bred to
Nan (D. Murray) ——— bred to ——— Cap 3036 (J. M. Wilson) ——— bred to
produced
Tib (E. W. Warwick)
bred to
Fleet (J. Relph)
produced
**PAT 4203, 1951** (A. E. Priestley)

produced
Nell (John Kirk)
bred to
Glen (W. J. Hislop)
produced
**GLEN 3940, 1946 & 1948** (J. M. Wilson)

bred to
Ben (G. P. Brown)
produced
Spot I (G. P. Brown)
bred to
Old Fly (Tho. Hunter)
produced
Scott (T. Brown)
bred to
Floss (John Jones)
produced
Jaff I (John Jones)
bred to
Queen (J. Morris)
produced
**JAFF II 2199, 1935** (John Jones)

bred to
Hemp 153 (T. Dickson)
produced
**FLY 824, 1928** (J. M. Wilson)

bred to
Old Fly (Tho. Hunter)
produced
Moss (C. B. Macpherson)
bred to
Meg (G. Lauder)
produced
**GLEN, 1926** (Mark Hayton)
bred to
Meg (A. Watson)
produced
**JESS, 1931** (John Thorp)

**Names in bold capitals indicate International Supreme Champions**

12

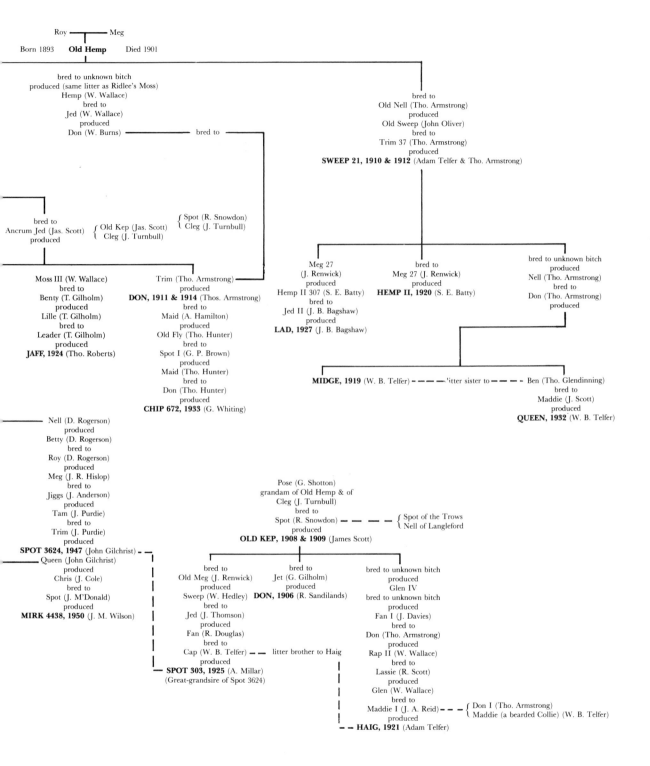

# Pedigree Chart Showing Breeding lines of International Sheep Dog Society Supreme Champions to 1951*

* Adapted from the pedigree chart given in *Border Collie Studies* by J. H. McCulloch

*Loos II 435*

main line. All descended from Hemp, and yet so wisely were these outstanding dogs bred, that the strength and beauty, the quality of their unique working method, and the health of the breed are as sound today as ever.

James A. Reid, secretary of the International Sheep Dog Society for thirty-two years and founder of the Stud Book, became involved in the breeding of the sheepdog, and was instrumental in exporting many of the best dogs of the day, particularly to Australia and New Zealand. It was he who bred Loos II 435, 'The Mother of Champions', herself a successful trial dog. She was owned by Wm. Wallace, Fingland, and bred many champions, including J. M. Wilson's Roy 1665, Supreme Champion three times, and Nicky 1823, who was Scottish National Champion and International

Farmers' Champion prior to being exported to Australia, both being by Craig 1048, a son of Hemp 153.

Loos II, a great-great-granddaughter of Tommy, bred particularly well to T. Dickson's Hemp 153, himself a great-grandson of Tommy, and bred by Adam Telfer, senior. J. M. Wilson's Supreme Champion, Fly 824, and his Nell 1627, three times Scottish National Champion, were from Loos II and Hemp 153.

The most famous daughter of J. M. Wilson's Cap 3036 was J. Kirk's Nell 3514, a great-granddaughter of Loos II. Nell's sons included J. M. Wilson's twice Supreme Champion Glen 3940 and Moss 5176, and W. J. Hislop's Sweep 3834. At Worcester in 1948, these three dogs were first, second and third in the Supreme Championship.

14

# The Supreme Champions
## 1906–95

**Black & white**  **R. Sandilands, Queensferry**

**Pedigree Details**

KEP 13, J. Scott ⎡SPOT – , R. Snowdon, Longwitton
⎣CLEG – , Turnbull

JET – , G. Gilholm ⎡Not known
⎣Not known

KEP 13 *International Supreme Champion 1908 & 1909*

## MOSS 22

**Black & white**     **W. Wallace, Otterburn**
**Exported to New Zealand and**
**became known as BORDER BOSS**

### Pedigree Details

| | | |
|---|---|---|
| **TOMMY 16, I. Herdman** | ┌ TWEED 246, W. Wallace | ┌ MOSS, R. Ridlie<br>└ OLD NELL, T. Armstrong |
| | └ GYP –, W. Wallace | ┌ Not known<br>└ Not known |
| **ANCRUM JED –, J. Renwick** | ┌ KEP 13, J. Scott | ┌ SPOT, R. Snowdon<br>└ CLEG, Turnbull |
| | └ CLEG –, J. Turnbull | ┌ Not known<br>└ Not known |

## KEP 13

**Black & white**     **J. Scott, Ancrum**
**Born 1901**

### Pedigree Details

| | |
|---|---|
| **SPOT – , R. Snowdon, Longwitton** | SPOT OF THE TROWS<br>NELL OF LANGLEFORD |
| **CLEG – , J. Turnbull** | Not known<br>Not known |

AULD KEP – for this is now his familiar name – the winner for the second time of the International Cup, is an average-sized dog of the type of the old Border Collie. He is finely coupled, and in action shows to great advantage at the sheep-dog trials. When he leaves his master to take command, there is an ease and confidence revealed that instantly stop the flow of speculations. The sheep seem at once to recognise his kindly powers, and, instead of rebelling, comply with his every request. Having an extremely strong eye, he at close quarters throws a mesmeric influence over both sheep and spectators. Now well accustomed to the trial course, he keeps perfectly cool, carefully scans the ground before beginning, and then lends an attentive ear to his master, and to his master only, no matter the excitement and noise beyond. When scarcely a year old he came to Mr Scott's hands, having then a deal to learn. He has won considerably over £200 in prize money, besides cups and medals. Today all authorities recognise him as the greatest sheepdog living.

That true working blood courses through his veins, is shown by the fact that his sons and daughters filled the entire prize list at the late sheep-dog trials at Perth on September 18. He is now eight years old.

*By Ralph Fleesh from A. L. J. Gosset,* Shepherds of Britain, *1911, p.154*

## To a Champion Dead

The light is dimmed in your loyal eyes,
Your swift white feet in the grass are still;
No more, old champion, wary and wise,
Shall you gather your sheep upon Troneyhill!
No more shall you scatter the morning dew
As you make your cast with the rising sun;
But the shepherd world shall remember you
As long as a dog on the hill shall run!

For those who have seen you stoop and fly
Like an arrow loosed from an archer's hand,
Hold your sheep with that masterful eye,
Crouch and creep at the least command –
Those who have watched you 'drive' and 'pen',
'Shed' and 'wear', on a stubborn three –
Have seen what never on earth again
The lover of dogs may be spared to see!

The short, sharp word of command shall pass
When the sheep in the show-ring turn and break
But no white breast shall gleam in the grass
As, alert, your answering turn you take.
Trophy and cup in the cottage stand,
Triumphs you won o'er the sheep-world's best;
But what shall they solace that lonely hand,
Champion Kep, that your tongue caressed?

Over your grave when the hill winds blow,
Kep, old Kep, will you hear the cheers,
The ringing plaudits you learned to know
In those glorious full-lived champion years?
Over your grave as the night-dews fall
Will they bring you a memory kind and true
Of the master who loved you better than all
And faced the world with his pride of you?

*Will. H. Ogilvie*

# SWEEP 21

**Black & white**     **A. Telfer, Morpeth**
**Exported to New Zealand**

### Awards
*International Supreme Champion 1912*

### Pedigree Details

| | | |
|---|---|---|
| SWEEP –, J. Oliver | HEMP 9, A. Telfer | ROY, A. Telfer<br>MEG, A. Telfer |
| | OLD NELL, T. Armstrong | Not known<br>Not known |
| TRIM 37, T. Armstrong | TOMMY 16, I. Herdman | TWEED 246, W. Wallace<br>GYP, W. Wallace |
| | JED –, J. Scott | Not known<br>Not known |

# DON 17

**Born –/7/09   Black & white     T. Armstrong, Otterburn**
**Exported to New Zealand**

## Awards
*International Supreme Champion 1914*

### Pedigree Details

|  |  |  |
|---|---|---|
| **DON –, W. Burns** | ⌐HEMP, W. Wallace | ⌐Not known<br>└Not known |
|  | └JED, W. Wallace | ⌐Not known<br>└Not known |
| **TRIM 37, T. Armstrong** | ⌐TOMMY 16, I. Herdman | ⌐TWEED 246, W. Wallace<br>└GYP, W. Wallace |
|  | └JED –, J. Scott | ⌐Not known<br>└Not known |

# SWEEP 21

**Black & white      T. Armstrong, Otterburn**
**Exported to New Zealand**

### Awards
*International Supreme Champion 1910*

### Pedigree Details

| | | |
|---|---|---|
| | ┌HEMP 9, A. Telfer | ┌ROY, A. Telfer<br>└MEG, A. Telfer |
| SWEEP –, J. Oliver | └OLD NELL, T. Armstrong | ┌Not known<br>└Not known |
| | ┌TOMMY 16, I. Herdman | ┌TWEED 246, W. Wallace<br>└GYP, W. Wallace |
| TRIM 37, T. Armstrong | └JED –, J. Scott | ┌Not known<br>└Not known |

# LAD 19

**Black, white & mottled**  **T. P. Brown, Oxton**
**Exported to New Zealand**

## Pedigree Details

| | | |
|---|---|---|
| **TOMMY 16, I. Herdman** | ┌TWEED 246, W. Wallace | ┌MOSS, R. Ridlie<br>└OLD NELL, T. Armstrong |
| | └GYP –, W. Wallace | ┌HEMP 9, A. Telfer<br>└FAN, Green |
| **OLD MAID 1, A. Brown** | ┌DON –, A. Renwick | ┌Not known<br>└Not known |
| | └NELL –, T. P. Brown | ┌Not known<br>└Not known |

# DON 17

**Born –/7/09    Black & white    T. Armstrong, Otterburn**
**Exported to New Zealand**

**Awards**

*International Supreme Champion 1911*

**Pedigree Details**

| | | |
|---|---|---|
| DON –, W. Burns | HEMP, W. Wallace | Not known<br>Not known |
| | JED, W. Wallace | Not known<br>Not known |
| TRIM 37, T. Armstrong | TOMMY 16, I. Herdman | TWEED 246, W. Wallace<br>GYP, W. Wallace |
| | JED –, J. Scott | Not known<br>Not known |

# No trials were held during the war years, 1915–18

# MIDGE 152

**Born –/7/18     Black & white     W. Telfer, Morpeth**

**Awards**

*International Farmers' Champion 1920 & 1921*

**Pedigree Details**

|  |  |  |
|---|---|---|
| **DON 17, T. Armstrong** | ┌DON – , W. Burns | ┌HEMP, W. Wallace └JED, W. Wallace |
|  | └TRIM 37, T. Armstrong | ┌TOMMY 16, I. Herdman └JED, J. Scott |
| **NELL – , T. Armstrong** | ┌SWEEP 21, T. Armstrong | ┌SWEEP, J. Oliver └TRIM 37, T. Armstrong |
|  | └Not known | ┌Not known └Not known |

**DON 17**  *International Supreme Champion 1911 & 1914*
**SWEEP 21**  *International Supreme Champion 1910 & 1912*

# HEMP 307

**Born 1912    Black & white     S. E. Batty, Sheffield**

## Pedigree Details

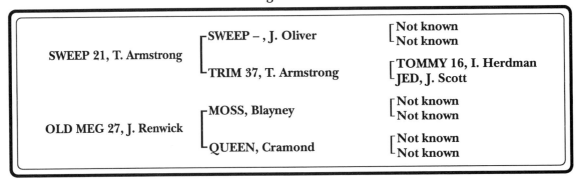

| | | |
|---|---|---|
| SWEEP 21, T. Armstrong | SWEEP – , J. Oliver | Not known / Not known |
| | TRIM 37, T. Armstrong | TOMMY 16, I. Herdman / JED, J. Scott |
| OLD MEG 27, J. Renwick | MOSS, Blayney | Not known / Not known |
| | QUEEN, Cramond | Not known / Not known |

**SWEEP 21**    *International Supreme Champion 1910 & 1912*

# HAIG 252

Born –/7/18   Black, white & tan   A. Telfer, Stampfordham

**Awards**

*English National Champion 1924*

**Pedigree Details**

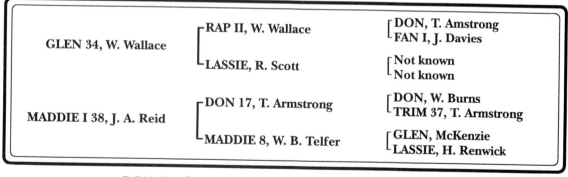

| | | |
|---|---|---|
| **GLEN 34, W. Wallace** | RAP II, W. Wallace | DON, T. Amstrong<br>FAN I, J. Davies |
| | LASSIE, R. Scott | Not known<br>Not known |
| **MADDIE I 38, J. A. Reid** | DON 17, T. Armstrong | DON, W. Burns<br>TRIM 37, T. Armstrong |
| | MADDIE 8, W. B. Telfer | GLEN, McKenzie<br>LASSIE, H. Renwick |

DON 17   *International Supreme Champion 1911 & 1914*

NOT ONLY is the name Telfer famed for breeding Hemp 9, 'Father' of the modern Border Collie, but also the family was renowned for the training and handling of sheepdogs. Adam senior won the Supreme Championship twice, was International Farmers' Champion with Toss 151, in 1919, and was English National Champion with Haig in 1924, when sons Walter and Adam were also members of the English team.

Walter won the Supreme Championship twice with bitches Midge and Queen, who also won the English National title three times. He was also International Farmers' Champion with Midge in 1920 and 1921, with Speed 366 in 1922 and with Queen in 1927.

27

## MEG 306

Born –/3/20　Black & white　W. Wallace, Otterburn

### Pedigree Details

| | | |
|---|---|---|
| TIP –, W. Amos | RAP, W. Wallace | Not known |
| | | Not known |
| | NELL II, J. Hedley | TYNE 145, I. Herdman |
| | | JED, Hedley |
| Nell III, J. Hedley | Not known | Not known |
| | | Not known |
| | Not known | Not known |
| | | Not known |

WILLIAM WALLACE, Otterburn, was fortunate to win the 1922 Supreme Championship, because Meg was stolen five days after the English National but was recovered in time for the International. As a lad, his son, W. J. Wallace, was allowed to run Meg at a Kelso trial, and unaccountably she deliberately put her sheep in the River Tweed, swam round them, brought them back onto the field and completed her course, winning third prize! It was with Meg's granddaughter, Jed, that W. J. Wallace won the Supreme Championship in 1938, and he was also reserve Supreme Champion with Foch 2344, a great-grandson of Meg, in the same year.

In 1909 William Wallace exported Moss to James Lilico in New Zealand, who declared him to be 'the greatest stud dog he ever had and one of the most perfect workers ever seen south of the Equator.' Trained by a great master, Moss, known as Border Boss in New Zealand, was easily handled, coolness being one of his strong points. He clapped too much to suit colonial taste but never turned tail no matter how hard-pressed. Always keeping well back, he never hustled his sheep and was always in the right place to keep them on line.

Shepherds, seeing Wm. Wallace's quiet handling of his dogs, began to improve their methods, and it is perhaps to him more than anyone else that we owe this style of sheepdog handling.

W. J. Wallace continued his father's 'family' of dogs. Hemp 4504, a son of Foch, was sire of Trim 5749, who partnered Hemp 6486 to win the 1953 English Brace Championship. The line of brood bitches bred by R. Gwilliam, Craven Arms, for the past forty years can be traced directly back to Hemp 4504. W. J. Wallace was well known for exhibitions at agricultural shows with his team of eight Border Collies.

# SPOT 308

**Born 1920  Black & white  G. P. Brown, Oxton**
**Exported to Sam Stoddart in the**
**United States**

## Awards

*International Shepherds' Champion 1922*
*Scottish National Champion 1923*

## Pedigree Details

|  |  |  |
|---|---|---|
| BEN 249, G. P. Brown | ┌DON 217, C. Hardisty | ┌DON 17, T. Armstrong └MEG 27, J. Renwick |
|  | └FAN 208, G. P. Brown | ┌TOMMY 16, I. Herdman └NELL 205, T. P. Brown |
| RUBY 207, G. P. Brown | ┌SKIP –, J. McKnight | ┌Not known └Not known |
|  | └MOSS –, A. Harrison | ┌Not known └Not known |

**DON 17** *International Supreme Champion 1911 & 1914*

# JAFF 379

**Born –/6/21    Black & white    T. Roberts, Corwen**

### Awards
*Welsh National Champion 1923 & 1924*

### Pedigree Details

|  |  |  |
|---|---|---|
| **LEADER 666, T. Gilholm** | ┌**KEP 13, J. Scott** | ┌SPOT, R. Snowdon └CLEG, J. Turnbull |
|  | └**LASSIE 518, T. Gilholm** | ┌HAIG 252, A. Telfer └JET 352, T. Gilholm |
| **LILLE 26, T. Gilholm** | ┌**MOSS III 28, W. Wallace** | ┌MOSS, Turnbull └LASSIE, W. Scott |
|  | └**BENTY – , Gilholm** | ┌Not known └Not known |

**KEP 13**   *International Supreme Champion 1908 & 1909*
**HAIG 252**   *International Supreme Champion 1921*
*English National Champion 1924*

## POINTS.

## QUALIFYING CLASSES. Friday, 26th September, 1924.

Competitors Selected at Society's National Trials at Haddington, Newcastle, and Talybont-on-Ursk.

| No. | COMPETITOR | Country and Class. | Stud Book No. | Dogs Name. | Class. | Ages Yrs. | Ages Mths. | Sire. | Dam | | GATHERING. | | | | Shedding 5 | Penning 5 | Single 5 | Style 5 | Command 10 | TOTAL TIME 55 |
|---|---|---|---|---|---|---|---|---|---|---|---|---|---|---|---|---|---|---|---|---|
| | | | | | | | | | | Outrun 5 | Lifting 5 | Bringing 5 | Driving 10 | | | | | | |
| 1 | A. Millar, High Bowhill, Newmilns, | Scot. | 526 | Jess | F | 1 | 4 | Kep, Wilson | Fly, Weir | | | | | | | | | | |
| 2 | David Henderson, Linthills, Lochwinnoch, | ,, | 167 | Nell | S | 8 | 4 | Tommy, Gilholm | Lille, Gilholm | | | | | | | | | | |
| 3 | C. B. M'Pherson, Balavil, Kingussie, | ,, | 454 | Moss | F | 2 | 10 | Spot, Braun | Fly, Hunter | | | | | | | | | | |
| 4 | Ben Murray, Farden Mulloch, Sanquhar, | ,, | 181 | Hemp | S | 6 | 3 | Ken, Wallace | Trim, Hunter | | | | | | | | | | |
| 5 | Thomas Dickson, Greenfield, Crawfordjohn, | ,, | 153 | Hemp | F | 7 | 0 | Yirrow, Telfer | Fenwick Jed, Telfer | | | | | | | | | | |
| 6 | Hugh Craig, Mark of Lochronald, Glenluce, | ,, | 264 | Moss | F | 6 | 2 | Rab, M'Inally | Bessie, M'Inally | | | | | | | | | | |
| 7 | Mark Hayton, Clifton, Otley, Yorks, | Eng. | 240 | Wylie | F | 5 | 0 | Moss, Renwick | Nell, Hedley | | | | | | | | | | |
| 8 | S. J. Davison, Sturton Grange, Warkworth, Morpeth, | ,, | 482 | Trim | S | 4 | 1 | Speed, Robson | Fan, Thomson | | | | | | | | | | |
| 9 | A. Telfer, jun, Great Law, Capheaton, | ,, | 534 | Jess | F | 1 | 4 | Wag, Hall | Beat, Dickenson | | | | | | | | | | |
| 10 | Mark Hayton (above), | ,, | 362 | Mac | F | 3 | 4 | Kep, Bell | Tip, Yates | | | | | | | | | | |
| 11 | John K. Young, Donkin Ridge, Cambio, Morpeth, | ,, | 471 | Moss | F | 4 | 11 | Dick, Laverne | Tibby, J. K. Young | | | | | | | | | | |
| 12 | Ernest Priestly, Boothsedge Farm, Hathersage, | ,, | 233 | Moss | F | 6 | 0 | Laddie, Rutherford | Fly, Hunter | | | | | | | | | | |
| 13 | J. Griffiths, Drysul, Crynent, near Recoh, | Wales | 551 | Fly | S | 3 | 5 | — | — | | | | | | | | | | |
| 14 | L. J. Humphreys, Rhoslefain Farm, Towyn, | ,, | 464 | Toss | F | 2 | 1 | Sweep, Hunter | Fly, Dickson | | | | | | | | | | |
| 15 | H. C. Darbishire, Naes-y-ewm, Llanalhairn, | ,, | 458 | Chris | F | 2 | 6 | Laddie, Reid | Merry, Darbishire | | | | | | | | | | |
| 16 | John Pritchard, Biaenau Canol, Liithfaen, | ,, | 406 | Laddie | F | 3 | 8 | Sweep, Hunter | Fan, T. Gilholm | | | | | | | | | | |
| 17 | Wm. Pritchard, Bwlch, Liithfaen, | ,, | 462 | Marry | S | 2 | 4 | Laddie, Reid | Marry, Darbishire | | | | | | | | | | |
| 18 | Hugh Pritchard, Nant Pach, Trevor, Chwilog, | ,, | 409 | Sprig | F | 3 | 6 | Boy, M'Pherson | Lille, Gilholm | | | | | | | | | | |

**INTERVAL FOR LUNCHEON.**

| No. | COMPETITOR | Country and Class. | Stud Book No. | Dogs Name. | Class. | Ages Yrs. | Ages Mths. | Sire. | Dam |
|---|---|---|---|---|---|---|---|---|---|
| 19 | Wm. Wallace, Fingland, Dalry, Galloway, | Scot. | 435 | Loos | F | 3 | 0 | Laddie, Reid | Loos, Reid |
| 20 | W. B. Telfer, Fairnley, Cambo, Morpeth, | Eng. | 532 | Sweep | F | 1 | 8 | Sweep, Landells | Nell, — |
| 21 | H. C. Darbishire (above), | Wales | 336 | Merry | F | 4 | 3 | Glen, Jr., Anderson | Fly, Hunter |
| 22 | Thos. Hunter, Glenburnie, Oxton, Berwickshire, | Scot. | 164 | Sweep | S | 6 | 2 | Laddie, Rutherford | Fly, Hunter |
| 23 | J. B. Bagshaw, The Mantles, Blyth, Rotherham, | Eng. | 305 | Lad | F | 4 | 2 | Hemp, Batty | Jed, Bagshaw |
| 24 | John Evans, Ty Newydd, Henrhyd, Conway, | Wales | 391 | Don | S | 3 | 5 | Kep, Bell | Tip, Yates |
| 25 | Robert Douglas, Dykeraw, Hawick, | Scot. | 519 | Tib | S | 1 | 8 | Spot, Braun | Fan, Douglas |
| 26 | Wm. Wallace, East Otterburn, Otterburn, | Eng. | 536 | Jean | F | 2 | 0 | Ben, Glendinning | Queen, Glendinning |
| 27 | John Evans (above), | Wales | 554 | Floss | S | 1 | 3 | Don, Evans | Jed, Evans |
| 28 | Thomas Dickson (above), | Scot. | 350 | Foozle | F | 0 | 0 | Hemp, Dickson | Lille, Gilholm |
| 29 | Wm. Wallace, Otterburn (above), | Eng. | 306 | Meg | F | 4 | 0 | Tip Amos | Maid, Bell |
| 30 | John Pritchard (above), | Wales | 552 | Spotan | F | 0 | 11 | Laddie, Pritchard | Nell, Pritchard |
| 31 | A. Miller (above), | Scot. | 303 | Spot | F | 3 | 6 | Cap, Telfer | Nan, Douglas |
| 32 | W. B. Telfer (above), | Eng. | 533 | Queen | F | 1 | 4 | Ben, Glendinning | — Scott |
| 33 | T. Roberts, Ty Cerrig, Bryneglwys, Corwen, | Wales | 467 | Moss | F | 3 | 0 | Spot, Braun | Fly, Hunter |
| 34 | A. Millar (above) (Scottish Cup Winner), | Scot. | 155 | Tot | F | 8 | 0 | Risp, Millar | Nancy, Millar |
| 35 | Adam Telfer, Capleaton (above, Eng. Cup Winner), | Eng. | 252 | Haig | F | 6 | 0 | Glen, Wallace | Maddie, Reid |
| 36 | T. Roberts, Corwen (above), (Welsh Cup Winner), | Wales | 379 | Juff | F | 3 | 3 | Leader, Gilholm | Lille, Gilholm |

32

# SPOT 303

**Born —/3/21    Black & white    A. Millar, Newmilns**

**Awards**

*Scottish National Champion 1922, 1925, 1926 & 1927*

**Pedigree Details**

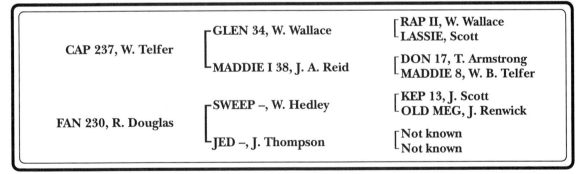

| | | |
|---|---|---|
| CAP 237, W. Telfer | GLEN 34, W. Wallace | RAP II, W. Wallace<br>LASSIE, Scott |
| | MADDIE I 38, J. A. Reid | DON 17, T. Armstrong<br>MADDIE 8, W. B. Telfer |
| FAN 230, R. Douglas | SWEEP –, W. Hedley | KEP 13, J. Scott<br>OLD MEG, J. Renwick |
| | JED –, J. Thompson | Not known<br>Not known |

**DON 17**  *International Supreme Champion 1911 & 1914*

'THE BIG MAN', Alex Millar, who was over six foot tall, was the first competitor to go to the post, with Frisk, at the first International at Gullane in 1906. On the trials field he became a great rival of J. M. Wilson, and he won nine Scottish Nationals, seven of them consecutively: with Spot 303, the 1925 Supreme Champion, in 1922, 1925, 1926 and 1927; with Tot 155 in

33

1924; with Mirk 836 in 1928 and 1929; and with Ben 891 in 1930. Ken 1477 was National Champion in 1934, when he also won the International and Scottish Aggregate Championships, and was also International Farmers' Champion, which title was won in 1928 and 1930 by Ben 891. Alex Millar won the International Brace Championship with Mirk 836 and Ben 891 in 1929, 1931 and 1932, Mirk and Ben also being Scottish Brace Champions in 1932. In 1946 he again won this award with Jock 4410 and Ben 4411, and the Scottish Driving Championship with Ben 4411 in 1949.

His son, J. R. Millar, was also a successful handler, winning four Scottish Nationals, with Drift 4380 in 1947; Ben 4931 in 1949; Tam 7032 in 1953 and Ken II 18754 in 1969. With Ben 12262 in 1960 he was International Farmers' Champion and won the Scottish Aggregate Championship, which award he had previously won in 1952 with Speed 4382. He was Scottish Brace Champion with Tam 7032 and Jim 10503 in 1955, and won the Scottish Driving Championship in 1946 and 1957 with Drift 4380 and Ben 12262, respectively.

J. R. Millar's son, Alex, has also competed at National level.

*Alex Millar with his half-beardie Frisk*

# GLEN 698

**Born –/4/24    Black, white & tan     M. Hayton, Otley**
**Exported to New Zealand**

## Pedigree Details

|  |  |  |
|---|---|---|
| **MOSS 454, C. B. McPherson** | ⌐SPOT I 308, G. P. Brown | ⌐BEN 249, G. P. Brown<br>└RUBY 207, G. P. Brown |
|  | └FLY 165, T. Hunter | ⌐DON, A. Hamilton<br>└MAID 945, A. Hamilton |
| **MEG 57, G. Lauder** | ⌐Not known | ⌐Not known<br>└Not known |
|  | └Not known | ⌐Not known<br>└Not known |

**SPOT I 308**    *International Supreme Champion 1923*

YORKSHIRE farmer Mark Hayton's 1926 Supreme Champion, Glen, was just twenty months old and in his first competitive season when he won this great award. Three years later he was exported to New Zealand, and only nine days after being out of quarantine he won the premier event in the New Zealand Championships. Mark Hayton was International Farmers' Champion in 1936 with Pat 2219, who won the English National Championship in 1937, and the English Aggregate Championship in 1936 and 1937. Sadly, Pat was stolen and never heard of again.

R. Gwilliams' foundation bitch Wattie 3272 was by Pat 2219, and mated to J. M. Wilson's Cap 3036 she produced Susan 4046, who was bred to W. J. Wallace's Hemp 4504; these two lines blended to produce the sound working dogs of the well-known 'Clun' prefix.

Mark Hayton wrote the following words — as true today as they were fifty years ago. 'It is not by the boot, the stick, the kennel and chain that a dog can be trained, or made man's loyal friend, but only by love. For those who understand, no explanation is needed; for those who do not, no explanation will prevail.'

His son Arthur, as successful a sheepdog handler as his father, was International Shepherds' and English Shepherds' Champion in 1934 with Pattie 1515, Glen's daughter, and in 1937 with Jock 2029, who was also English Shepherds' Champion in 1935, 1936 and 1939, while Pattie won this award again in 1938. Pattie and Jock were English Brace Champions in 1935. Barney 4365, a son of Paddie 4364 and Mark Hayton's Pat 2219, was the 1947 English National Champion, and he and Paddie won the 1946 International Brace Championship.

# LAD 305

**Born –/4/20    Black & tan    J. B. Bagshaw, Rotherham**

### Awards

*International Farmers' Champion 1926*
*English National Champion 1925*

### Pedigree Details

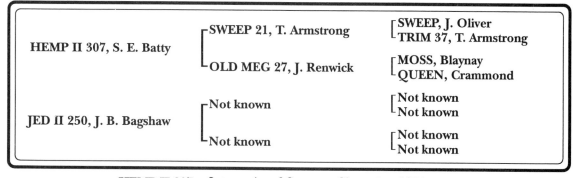

**HEMP II 307**   *International Supreme Champion 1920*
**SWEEP 21**   *International Supreme Champion 1910 & 1912*

J. B. BAGSHAW, much involved with the organisation of the Longshaw trials, where he was also a successful competitor, won the 1925 English National Championship with his 1927 Supreme Champion, Lad, who was also International Farmers' Champion in 1926. His Moss 569 was English National Champion in 1931.

W. B. Bagshaw, like his father, was a well-known handler, winning the English National Championship in 1928 and in 1932 with Jess 818, a daughter of T. Roberts' 1924 Supreme Champion, Jaff, and again in 1946 with Mac 4418, son of Mark Hayton's Pat 2219.

# FLY 824

**Born 28/2/26    Black & white    J. M. Wilson, Moffat**

## Awards

*International Farmers' Champion 1931*
*Scottish Brace Champion with Craig 1048, 1931*
*Scottish Brace Champion with Nell 1627, 1933*
*Scottish Brace Champion with Roy 1665, 1934*

## Pedigree Details

| | | |
|---|---|---|
| **HEMP 153, T. M. Dickson** | ┌ YARROW 23, A. Telfer | ┌ TYNE 145, I. Herdman<br>└ NELL (MEG), J. Renwick |
| | └ FENWICK JED 33, A. Telfer | ┌ MOSS, A. Telfer<br>└ WYLIE, G. Snaith |
| **LOOS II 435, W. Wallace** | ┌ LADDIE 317, J. A. Reid | ┌ ROY, Hindmarsh<br>└ JED, Hindmarsh |
| | └ LOOS I – , J. A. Reid | ┌ TOM, T. Gilholm<br>└ LILLE 26, T. Gilholm |

**HEMP 153**   *International Farmers' Champion 1924*
**LOOS II 435**   *International Farmers' Champion 1925*

# CORBY 338

**Born –/3/20    Black, white & tan      S. E. Batty, Worksop**

## Pedigree Details

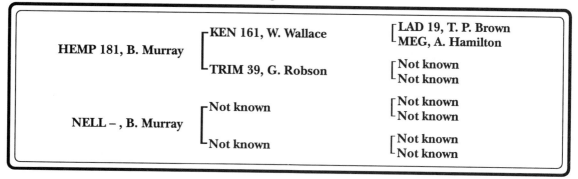

| | KEN 161, W. Wallace | LAD 19, T. P. Brown |
|---|---|---|
| HEMP 181, B. Murray | | MEG, A. Hamilton |
| | TRIM 39, G. Robson | Not known |
| | | Not known |
| | Not known | Not known |
| NELL – , B. Murray | | Not known |
| | Not known | Not known |
| | | Not known |

**LAD 19**  *International Supreme Champion 1913*

*S. E. Batty with Corby 338*

# CRAIG 1048

**Born 8/6/27    Black & white    J. M. Wilson, Moffat**

### Awards
*International Farmers' Champion 1929*
*Scottish National Champion 1931 & 1932*
*Scottish Brace Champion with Fly 824, 1931*
*International Aggregate Championship 1932*

### Pedigree Details

| | | |
|---|---|---|
| **HEMP 153, T. M. Dickson** | ┌YARROW 23, A. Telfer | ┌TYNE 145, I. Herdman<br>└NELL (MEG), J. Renwick |
| | └FENWICK JED 33, A. Telfer | ┌MOSS, A. Telfer<br>└WYLIE, G. Snaith |
| **MIST 332, A. Craig** | ┌CAP 237, W. B. Telfer | ┌GLEN 34, W. Wallace<br>└MADDIE I 38, J. A. Reid |
| | └FLY 221, J. F. J. Wilson | ┌GLEN 34, W. Wallace<br>└JED 220, J. F. Wilson |

**HEMP 153**   *International Farmers' Champion 1924*

# JESS 1007

**Born –/6/27    Black, white & tan    J. Thorp, Sheffield**

## Awards

*International Farmers' Champion 1932*
*International Brace Champion with Meg 1179, 1936*
*English Brace Champion with Meg 1179, 1931 & 1932*

### Pedigree Details

| | | |
|---|---|---|
| **GLEN 698, M. Hayton** | ┌**MOSS 454, C. B. McPherson** | ┌**SPOT 308, G. P. Brown**<br>└**FLY 165, T. Hunter** |
| | └**MEG 57, G. Lauder** | ┌**Not known**<br>└**Not known** |
| **MEG 362, A. Watson** | ┌**LADDIE –, W. Glendinning** | ┌**Not known**<br>└**Not known** |
| | └**GYP – , T. Ridley** | ┌**Not known**<br>└**Not known** |

**GLEN 698**   *International Supreme Champion 1926*
**SPOT 308**   *International Shepehrds' Champion 1922*
            *Scottish National Champion 1923*

*J. Thorp with Jess 1007* (left) *and Meg 1179* (right)

# QUEEN 533

**Born –/4/25**    **Black & white**    **W. B. Telfer, Morpeth**

### Awards

*International Farmers' Champion 1927*
*English National Champion 1926, 1927 & 1929*

### Pedigree Details

| | | |
|---|---|---|
| **BEN 75, T. Glendinning** | ┌DON II – , T. Armstrong | ┌Not known<br>└Not known |
| | └NELL – , T. Armstrong | ┌Not known<br>└Not known |
| **MADDIE 69, J. Scott** | ┌DON 17, T. Armstrong | ┌DON, W. Burns<br>└TRIM 37, T. Armstrong |
| | └JEAN – , T. Dickson | ┌Not known<br>└Not known |

**DON 17**   *International Supreme Champion 1911 & 1914*

# CHIP 672

**Born 11/4/25    Black & white      G. Whiting, Aberdare**

**Awards**

*Welsh Shepherds' Champion 1937*
*International Aggregate Championship 1933*

**Pedigree Details**

| | | |
|---|---|---|
| **DON – , T. Hunter** | Not known | Not known<br>Not known |
| | Not known | Not known<br>Not known |
| **MAID 489, T. Hunter** | SPOT I 308, G. P. Brown | BEN 249, G. P. Brown<br>RUBY 207, G. P. Brown |
| | FLY 165, T. Hunter | DON, A. Hamilton<br>MAID 945, A. Hamilton |

**SPOT I 308**    *International Supreme Champion 1923*

# ROY 1665

**Born 7/4/31    Black & white    J. M. Wilson, Moffat**

### Awards

*International Farmers' Champion 1935*
*International Brace Champion with Nell 1627, 1937 & 1938*
*Scottish National Champion 1937*
*Scottish Brace Champion with Fly 824, 1934*
*Scottish Brace Champion with Nell 1627, 1936, 1937 & 1938*
*International Aggregate Championship 1936 & 1937*
*Scottish Aggregate Trophy 1936 & 1937*

### Pedigree Details

|  |  |  |
|---|---|---|
| CRAIG 1048, J. M. Wilson | ┌HEMP 153, T. M. Dickson | ┌YARROW 23, A. Telfer<br>└FENWICK JED 33, A. Telfer |
|  | └MIST 332, A. Craig | ┌CAP 237, W. B. Telfer<br>└FLY 221, J. F. Wilson |
| LOOS II 435, W. Wallace | ┌LADDIE 317, J. A. Reid | ┌ROY, Hindmarsh<br>└JED, Hindmarsh |
|  | └LOOS I – , J. A. Reid | ┌TOM, T. Gilholm<br>└LILLE 26, T. Gilholm |

**CRAIG 1048** *International Supreme Champion 1930*
**LOOS II 435** *International Farmers' Champion 1925*
**HEMP 153** *International Farmers' Champion 1924*

ROY'S cleverness is uncanny. He comes as near human intelligence as an animal can.

Yet at one time his master despaired of ever making him a star. His mother, Loos, belonging to Mr Wallace, Dalry, had won everything worthwhile at trials all over the country. So had Craig, his father, owned by Mr Wilson himself. Craig won the International blue riband at Ayr in 1930.

Everything pointed to Roy being a crack. But his master got a real disappointment when he started the dog's training. At four months he did not pick up the work as quickly as was expected. The instinct to herd sheep usually helps a collie to know what his master wants. Slowly and patiently Mr Wilson taught the dog his whistles, commands, and signals. But Roy was not enthusiastic. He was dour.

On top of that he took distemper, the dreaded scourge of dogdom. For days Roy hung between life and death. Gradually he regained strength, until once more his ears were cocked, his eyes bright. But still he refused to display a lively interest in sheep. Yet some day Mr Wilson knew breeding must out.

Then Roy and his half-brother, Jix, a famed performer, decided to settle a private quarrel. Roy lost the fight – and very nearly the sight of an eye. For a time he was quite blind. It looked as if his career was over before it had

begun. But, to his master's surprise, Roy recovered.

And from that moment he was a greatly improved puppy. He began to shed sheep as well as Craig, a master in that craft. He developed his mother's handsome looks and ability to drive. 'He will never fall back into his old ways,' declared Mr Wilson. 'He's learned his job – and he'll never forget it. Nothing puts him off. Even if a gun-shot is heard during a trial he never flicks an ear. But if I whistle him to lie down, he obeys on the instant.

'I have never struck him in my life. Indeed, I make a point of never hitting any of my dogs at any time. To make a dog have faith in you, you must treat him with kindness. Not that I am soft with Roy, of course. When I give him orders, I see he carries them out to the letter. But you can have discipline without using a stick.'

These trials apparently do not spoil collies for ordinary work. Roy works hard on the great, round-shouldered hills around his home. Mr Wilson stands in the glens while Roy brings down the sheep for miles around.

He is more to Mr Wilson than a crack performer. He has a place in his heart.

## V.

*Extract from newspaper article, 1934*

# JAFF II 2199

**Born 7/6/33   Black & white    J. Jones, Corwen**
**Exported to New Zealand**

**Awards**

*Welsh Aggregate Championship 1935*

## Pedigree Details

| | | |
|---|---|---|
| JAFF 1267, J. Jones | SCOT 564, E. Ll. Williams | SPOT 308, G. P. Brown<br>FLY 165, T. Hunter |
| | FLOSS 1245, E. P. Jones | JAFF 379, T. Roberts<br>DOLL, E. V. Jones |
| QUEEN 149, J. Morris | MOSS –, W. W. Lloyd | Not known<br>Not known |
| | LADY –, J. Morris | HOP, W. Jones<br>NELL, W. Morris |

**SPOT 308** *International Supreme Champion 1923*
*International Shepherds' Champion 1922*
*Scottish National Champion 1923*
**JAFF 379** *International Supreme Champion 1924*
*Welsh National Champion 1923 & 1924*

JOHN JONES, Corwen, having won the Supreme Championship with Jaff in 1935 and also the Welsh Aggregate Championship, also won the latter award with Fleet 2200, a son of T. Roberts' Jaff 379, in 1936.

His son, Meirion, won the Supreme Championship in 1959 with Ben 13879, and he had been a member of the Welsh team in 1956 and 1958, winning the Welsh Aggregate Championship with Tibbie 11113 in both years. Tibbie was third in the 1956 Supreme Championship and reserve Supreme Champion in 1958 to W. J. Evans' Tweed.

In 1966 Meirion was Welsh Farmers' Champion with Craig 28979. He won the Welsh Brace Championship in 1973 with Moss 58970 and Moss 56535, the latter dog being International Farmers' Champion in 1974, which award was won by Bill 108410 in 1984.

Meirion won the Welsh National, Welsh Farmers' and Welsh Driving Championships with Craig 67343 in 1979, and he also won the International Brace and International Brace Aggregate Championships with Craig and Ben 105608. With Bill 108410 and Cap 120298 he again won the International Brace and International Brace Aggregate Championships in 1986. The awards won with Supreme Champions Ben and Spot are listed in their individual entries.

## ROY 1665

**Born 7/4/31    Black & white    J. M. Wilson, MBE, Moffat**

### Awards

*International Farmers' Champion 1935*
*International Brace Champion with Nell 1627, 1937 & 1938*
*Scottish National Champion 1937*
*Scottish Brace Champion with Fly 824, 1934*
*Scottish Brace Champion with Nell 1627, 1936, 1937 & 1938*
*International Aggregate Championship 1936 & 1937*
*Scottish Aggregate Trophy 1936 & 1937*

## Pedigree Details

CRAIG 1048, J. M. Wilson
- HEMP 153, T. M. Dickson
  - YARROW 23, A. Telfer
  - FENWICK JED 33, A. Telfer
- MIST 332, A. Craig
  - CAP 237, W. B. Telfer
  - FLY 221, J. F. Wilson

LOOS II 435, W. Wallace
- LADDIE 317, J. A. Reid
  - ROY, Hindmarsh
  - JED, Hindmarsh
- LOOS I – , J. A. Reid
  - TOM, T. Gilholm
  - LILLE 26, T. Gilholm

**CRAIG 1048** *International Supreme Champion 1930*
**LOOS II 435** *International Farmers' Champion 1925*
**HEMP 153** *International Farmers' Champion 1924*

# JED I 1492

**Born 24/7/30    Black & white    W. J. Wallace, Otterburn**

## Awards

*International Brace Champion with Fly 1657, 1933 & 1934*
*English National Champion 1933*
*English Aggregate Championship 1938*
*International Aggregate Championship 1938*

## Pedigree Details

| | | |
|---|---|---|
| **MOSS IV 1009, W. Wallace** | ┌**NAP 434, A. E. Herdman** | ┌**GLEN, W. Wallace**<br>└**JED II, W. Cousin** |
| | └**MEG 306, W. Wallace** | ┌**TIP, W. Amos**<br>└**NELL, J. Hedley** |
| **MADDIE II – , A. Heslop** | ┌**MOSS, Blancy** | ┌**Not known**<br>└**Not known** |
| | └**MADDIE, A. Heslop** | ┌**Not known**<br>└**Not known** |

**MEG 306**    *International Supreme Champion 1922*

*W. J. Wallace with Jed I 1492* (left) *and Foch 2344* (right), *who was reserve champion*

**The 1939 National Trials were held, but not the International. No trials were held during the war years 1940–45.**

# GLEN 3940

**Born 15/9/43    Black & white    J. M. Wilson, Innerleithen**

### Awards
*International Supreme Champion 1948*
*International Farmers' Champion 1948*
*Scottish National Champion 1946*
*International Aggregate Championship 1946 & 1948*
*Scottish Aggregate Trophy 1946 & 1948*

## Pedigree Details

| | | |
|---|---|---|
| **GLEN 3510, W. Hislop** | ┌ **BEN 1572, A. Riddell** | ┌ **GLEN 603, T. Hunter**<br>└ **SLY 1087, P. Dignan** |
| | └ **BEAT I – , J. Guthrie** | ┌ **Not known**<br>└ **Not known** |
| **NELL 3514, J. Kirk** | ┌ **CAP 3036, J. M. Wilson** | ┌ **SAM 2336, H. Cullens**<br>└ **PEN 2572, H. Cullens** |
| | └ **MOSS 1827, McCaskie** | ┌ **MOSS 1677, A. Storie**<br>└ **NICKEY, T. M. Dickson** |

JAMES M. WILSON, MBE – the greatest sheep-dog handler of all time, a breeder of top-quality Scotch Blackface sheep, winner of nine International Supreme Championships, six International Farmers' Championships, two International Brace Championships, eleven Scottish National Championships and six Scottish Brace Championships – set a record that is never likely to be equalled.

Winning his first International with Fly 824 in 1928 at Llandudno, he was a force to be reckoned with until he retired from International competition after winning the Supreme Championship with Bill 9040 in 1955 at Edinburgh, after a masterly display of shedding.

Whitehope Nap 8685 was reserve champion, and the previous day these two dogs had been in the same positions in the qualifying trials. That year Whitehope Nap had won the Scottish National Championship with Bill in second place.

His Majesty King George V summoned

*J. M. Wilson with* (left to right)
*Tib, Pat, Cap, Phil, Nell and Roy*

*J. M. Wilson with* (left to right) *Tib, Glen, Mirk and Moss*

J. M. Wilson and Alex Millar to give the Royal Family a command performance of their Collies' skills at Balmoral. A most treasured possession was the gold pocket watch presented to J. M. Wilson by the King, who thought Craig the most beautiful Collie he had ever seen.

Roy 1665 is perhaps a legend in his own right, having survived a somewhat traumatic youth to become the only dog, to date, to have won the Supreme Championship three times.

Distemper was rife in those days and many of J. M. Wilson's dogs suffered this debilitating disease. Glen, twice International Champion, won at Edinburgh while recovering from it, and as his sight was affected, he competed in no further International competitions after winning again at Worcester in 1948.

Moss 5176, probably the unluckiest of his dogs, also suffered from distemper, as did his sire Mirk 4438. Twice Moss was reserve cham-

pion, to Glen in 1948 and to D. W. Daniels' Chip in 1949, and although he was doomed to be an also-ran, he was a much-sought-after stud dog.

The International Supreme Champions of J. M. Wilson are shown within these pages, but so great were his ISDS trials' successes that they are listed here.

The International Farmers' Championship was won in 1929 by Craig 1048, in 1931 by Fly 824, in 1933 by Nickey 1823, in 1935 by Roy 1665, in 1948 by Glen 3940 and in 1955 by Bill 9040.

Roy 1665 and Nell 1627 won the International Brace Championship in 1937 and 1938. The Scottish National was won by Craig 1048 in 1931 and 1932; by Nickey 1823 in 1933; by Nell 1627 in 1935, 1936 and 1939; by Roy 1665 in 1937; by Glen 3940 in 1946; by Mirk 4438 in 1950; by Tib 6903 in 1951; and by Whitehope Nap 8685 in 1955.

J. M. Wilson won the Scottish Brace Championship with Craig 1048 and Fly 824 in 1931; with Fly 824 and Nell 1627 in 1933; with Fly 824 and Roy 1665 in 1934; and with Roy 1665 and Nell 1627 in 1936, 1937 and 1938.

An unsurpassed record. And 1957 saw this great sheepdog handler honoured by Her Majesty the Queen with the MBE for his services to agriculture.

Cap 3036, a half-white-headed dog born in 1937, is perhaps one of the best known of J. M. Wilson's dogs, though he did not have the opportunity to prove his skills at ISDS trials, because these were not held during the war years. The fame of his superior working abilities on the home hills spread far and wide, and bitches were sent to him from all parts of Britain. Cap's most famous daughter was J. Kirk's Nell 3514, who was dam of J. M. Wilson's Glen and Moss, and also of W. J. Hislop's Sweep 3834. At the 1948 International Glen was Supreme Champion, with Moss second, and Sweep was third. There are few, if any, modern Border Collie pedigrees that do not contain Cap 3036, so he too has gained renown in keeping with his 'champion' kennel mates.

*J. M. Wilson with Cap 3036*

## SPOT 3624

**Born 16/4/43     Black & white     J. Gilchrist, Haddington**

### Awards

*International Brace Champion with Ben 5714, 1948*
*International Brace Champion with Glen 6425, 1949*
*Scottish Shepherds' Champion 1947*
*Scottish Brace Champion with Ben 5714, 1948*
*Scottish Brace Champion with Glen 6425, 1949*
*Scottish Driving Champion 1953*
*International Aggregate Championship 1947*
*Scottish Aggregate Trophy 1947*
*Scottish Shepherds' Aggregate Championship 1946 & 1947*

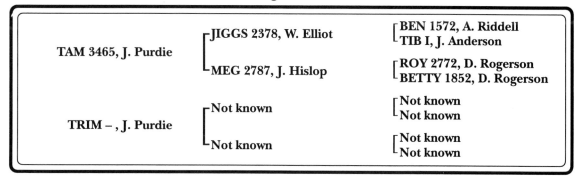

|  |  |  |
|---|---|---|
| TAM 3465, J. Purdie | JIGGS 2378, W. Elliot | BEN 1572, A. Riddell / TIB I, J. Anderson |
|  | MEG 2787, J. Hislop | ROY 2772, D. Rogerson / BETTY 1852, D. Rogerson |
| TRIM – , J. Purdie | Not known | Not known / Not known |
|  | Not known | Not known / Not known |

JOHN GILCHRIST, 1947 Supreme Champion with Spot 3624, nearly won the award again at Chester in 1966, when Spot 24981, a great-great-grandson of Spot 3624, was reserve to Supreme Champion Tim Longton's Ken. He won, too, the International Aggregate Championship. Earlier that year he had been Scottish National Champion and won the Scottish Shepherds' and Scottish Aggregate Championships. Spot also won the Scottish National and Shepherds' Championships in 1965.

In 1976 John Gilchrist and Bob 79686 won the Scottish Shepherds' Aggregate and Scottish Driving Championships. W. S. Hetherington's white bitch Ann 4545, great-great-grandam of Wiston Cap 31154 and in the pedigrees of many famous dogs, was a litter sister to Spot 3624.

James Gilchrist was a great breeder of Border Collies, though perhaps not so successful on the trials field as his brother. He won the 1964 Scottish Brace Championship with Spot 14019 and Glen 28313. With Mirk 47957 he won the 1970 Scottish Farmers' Championship and the 1973 Scottish Driving Championship, the latter of which he had won in 1971 with Tam 25605. Despite failing to pen he was fifth in the 1956 Supreme Championship with Spot 7320, a grandson of Spot 3624. Spot had that year been second in the Scottish National, beaten by half a point by T. Bonella's Moss 7878.

# GLEN 3940

**Born 15/9/43   Black & white   J. M. Wilson, Innerleithen**

### Awards

*International Supreme Champion 1946*
*International Farmers' Champion 1948*
*Scottish National Champion 1946*
*International Aggregate Championship 1946 & 1948*
*Scottish Aggregate Trophy 1946 & 1948*

### Pedigree Details

| | | |
|---|---|---|
| **GLEN 3510, W. Hislop** | ⌐BEN 1572, A. Riddell | ⌐GLEN 603, T. Hunter<br>└SLY 1087, P. Dignan |
| | └BEAT I – , J. Guthrie | ⌐Not known<br>└Not known |
| **NELL 3514, J. Kirk** | ⌐CAP 3036, J. M. Wilson | ⌐SAM 2336, H. Cullens<br>└PEN 2572, H. Cullens |
| | └MOSS 1827, McCaskie | ⌐MOSS 1677, A. Storie<br>└NICKEY, T. M. Dickson |

# CHIP 4924

**Born 1/3/46    Black & white    D. W. Daniel, Ystradgynlais**

### Awards

*International Supreme Champion 1952*
*Welsh Aggregate Championship 1949*

### Pedigree Details

| MOSS – , W. Elliott | Not known<br>Not known |
| --- | --- |
| TIB – , D. Dickson | TOSS, J. Scott<br>TRIM, D. Dickson |

D. W. DANIEL, winner of the Supreme Championship in 1949 and 1952 with Chip, was also Welsh Aggregate Champion in 1949 with Chip. He also won this same award in 1955 and 1957 with Floss 11400, and in 1958 he was International Farmers' Champion with Allan 12085, a son of Chip.

His son Eurwyn won the Supreme Championship in 1960 with Ken, a son of Chip and Floss, and in 1968 was reserve Supreme Champion with Ken's son, Chip 22797. This dog was International Aggregate Champion and also Welsh Driving Champion in 1968. Eurwyn Daniel won the Welsh Farmers' Championship in 1982 with Meg 96043 and in 1984 with Ken 101980.

D. K. Daniel, the third generation of successful handlers, has already been a member of the Welsh team on several occasions.

*E. L. Daniel with Meg 96043*

## MIRK 4438

**Born 19/4/44    Black & white     J. M. Wilson, Innerleithen**

### Awards
*Scottish National Champion 1950*
*International Aggregate Championship 1950*
*Scottish Aggregate Trophy 1950*

### Pedigree Details

| | | |
|---|---|---|
| **SPOT 3369, J. McDonald** | ┌MOSS – , W. Amos | ┌Not known<br>└Not known |
| | └MEG – , J. McDonald | ┌Not known<br>└Not known |
| **CHRIS 4065, J. Cole** | ┌CAP 3036, J. M. Wilson | ┌SAM 2336, H. Cullens<br>└PEN 2572, H. Cullens |
| | └QUEEN 3113, J. Gilchrist | ┌WATT, J. Gilchrist<br>└QUEEN, J. Gilchrist |

## PAT 4203

**Born 28/7/44    Black & white    E. A. Priestley, Bamford**

**Awards**
*International Farmers' Champion 1950*
*English Driving Champion 1951*
*English Brace Champion with Mac 8133, 1952*
*International Aggregate Championship 1951*
*English Aggregate Championship 1950 & 1951*
*Brace Aggregate Trophy with Mac 8133, 1952*

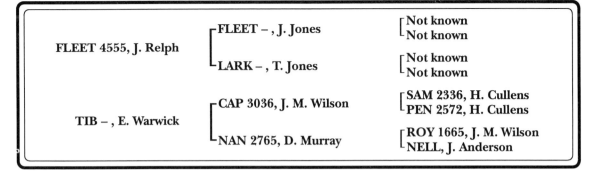

|  |  |  |  |
|---|---|---|---|
| **FLEET 4555, J. Relph** | ┌ FLEET – , J. Jones | ┌ Not known<br>└ Not known |  |
|  | └ LARK – , T. Jones | ┌ Not known<br>└ Not known |  |
| **TIB – , E. Warwick** | ┌ CAP 3036, J. M. Wilson | ┌ SAM 2336, H. Cullens<br>└ PEN 2572, H. Cullens |  |
|  | └ NAN 2765, D. Murray | ┌ ROY 1665, J. M. Wilson<br>└ NELL, J. Anderson |  |

**FLEET 4555**   *English Brace Champion 1948*

**ROY 1665**   *International Supreme Champion 1934, 1936 & 1937*
*International Farmers' Champion 1935*
*International Brace Champion 1937 & 1938*
*International & Scottish Aggregate Championships 1936 & 1937*
*Scottish Brace Champion 1934, 1936, 1937 & 1938*
*Scottish National Champion 1937*

LIVING in a remote house high on the Derbyshire moors, Ernest Priestley was one of the sheep men who began the famous Longshaw trials, competing in a challenge match in c. 1894, and the family have supported this trial ever since that first day. Longshaw trial became 'official' in 1898.

Ernest Priestley won the English National Championship with Moss 233 in 1922 and 1923, and with Hemp 1006 in 1930. His son, Ashton, handled Lad 859 and Wylie 1184 to win the International Brace Championship in 1930, and Lad and Hemp to win the English Brace Championship in 1933. Lad, Hemp and Wylie were bred from Ernest Priestley's Jet 607 by Dickson's Hemp 153.

Ashton won the Supreme Championship in 1951 with Pat 4203, who had been reserve to Supreme Champion J. M. Wilson's Mirk 4438 the previous year. Pat and Mac 8133 were English Brace Champions in 1952. With Jim 10071 and Sweep 11115 he won the English National Championships in 1955 and 1960, respectively. Malcolm Priestley, his son, is also a successful sheepdog handler, and Ashton's daughter is married to another famous trial man, Raymond MacPherson, who won the Supreme Championship twice with Zac.

# CHIP 4924

**Born 1/3/46    Black & white    D. W. Daniel, Ystradgynlais**

### Awards
*International Supreme Champion 1949*
*Welsh Aggregate Championship 1949*

### Pedigree Details

| | |
|---|---|
| **MOSS – , W. Elliott** | [ Not known<br>Not known |
| **TIB – , D. Dickson** | [ TOSS, J. Scott<br>TRIM, D. Dickson |

# ROY 7696

**Born 3/4/49    Black, white & tan    W. J. Evans, Magor**

## Awards

*International Brace Champion with Moss 7971, 1957*
*Welsh Brace Champion with Nell 6879, 1953*
*International Aggregate Championship 1953*
*Welsh Aggregate Championship 1953*
*Brace Aggregate Trophy with Moss 7971, 1957*

## Pedigree Details

| | | |
|---|---|---|
| **MAC 5498, J. Evans** | ┌JAFF 4313, R. J. Hughes | ┌COON 1608, Lord Mostyn<br>└NELL, T. O. Jones |
| | └MINN 3387, J C. Williams | ┌MOSS 4474, J. Gilchrist<br>└MEG 4374, W. Turnbull |
| **MEG 6782, G. Jones** | ┌GLEN 2584, J. Jones | ┌JAFF, E. G. Jones<br>└TRIM 2420, J. Jones |
| | └MON 3417, T. Jones | ┌SCOT, J. Williams<br>└MEG, H. Morgan |

**JAFF 4313** *International & Welsh Driving Champion 1946, 1947 & 1949*
*Welsh National Champion 1946 & 1948*
*Welsh Brace Champion 1946*
**MINN 3387** *Challis Shield 1952*

W. J. EVANS, besides being an excellent handler, was a superb showman, giving many exhibitions at agricultural shows with his team of trial winning dogs and with his Hungarian horse, Condor. Her Majesty the Queen commanded him to give an exhibition at Windsor before members of the Royal Family and their guest Haile Selassie, Emperor of Ethiopia.

While living in Wales, W. J. Evans won the Welsh National with Sweep 4204, in 1949, having previously been International Farmers' Champion in 1947 with Jaff 2885,

which title he again won with Nell 6879 in 1953 at Cardiff, when he also won the Supreme Championship with Roy 7696, who became a popular stud dog. Nell 6879 won the Welsh Brace Championships in partnership with Coon 5701 in 1951, with Roy 7696 in 1953 and with Moss 7971 in 1956. Roy 7696 and Moss 7971 won the 1957 International Brace Championship at Loughborough.

Then, going to reside in Gloucestershire, W. J. Evans proceeded to win the 1958 English National with Moss 7971, and to win the

*W. J. Evans with* (left to right) *Roy, Tweed and Moss*

68

*W. J. Evans with* (left to right) *Ben, Sandy, Tweed, Roy and Moss*

Supreme Championship a few weeks later at Dundee, with Tweed 9601, purchased earlier from J. M. Wilson, who had retired from International competition. He also won the English National Championship with Tweed 9601 in 1959, with Don 13392 in 1962 and with Ben 12953 in 1963. Don 13392 was also the 1962 International Farmers' Champion. Tweed 9601 in partnership with Moss 7971 won the English Brace Championship in 1958 and 1960.

# MIRK 5444

**Born 1/5/46    Black, white & tan    J. McDonald, Lauder**

**Awards**

*Scottish Shepherds' Aggregate Championship 1952*

**Pedigree Details**

|  |  |  |
|---|---|---|
| **REED – , Corbet** | ┌ Not known | ┌ Not known<br>└ Not known |
|  | └ Not known | ┌ Not known<br>└ Not known |
| **MADGE 5449, W. Cowan** | ┌ FOCH 2344, W. J. Wallace | ┌ ROGER 1277, W. Wallace<br>└ FLY 1657, W. J. Wallace |
|  | └ BETTY – , W. Cowan | ┌ Not known<br>└ Not known |

# BILL 9040

(Scottish Farmer)

**Born 21/6/51**    **Black & white**    **J. M. Wilson, Innerleithen**
**Exported to America, where he won the**
**North American Championship in 1958**

## Awards

*International Farmers' Champion 1955*
*International Aggregate Championship 1955*
*Scottish Aggregate Trophy 1955*

## Pedigree Details

| | | |
|---|---|---|
| **GARRY 4915, J. Anderson** | ┌**GLEN 3957, S. Banks** | ┌**GLEN 3510, W. J. Hislop**<br>└**NELL 3514, W. J. Hislop** |
| | └**TIB 4458, S. Banks** | ┌**SPOT 3369, J. McDonald**<br>└**LINT, C. Scott** |
| **QUEEN 8278, J. Kirk** | ┌**SWEEP 3834, W. J. Hislop** | ┌**GLEN 3510, W. J. Hislop**<br>└**NELL 3514, W. J. Hislop** |
| | └**LASSIE 6711, A. McCudden** | ┌**CAP 3036, J. M. Wilson**<br>└**TIB 2819, T. Brotherstone** |

**SWEEP 3834**    *International Farmers' Champion 1946*
                  *Scottish National Champion & Driving Champion 1948*

## MOSS 6805

*Moss 6805* (left) *and*
*Coon 9077* (right)

(Cyril Lindley)

**Born 10/12/48　Black & white　G. R. Redpath, Jedburgh**

### Awards

*International Shepherds' Champion 1952*
*Scottish Shepherds' Champion 1952 & 1956*
*Scottish Driving Champion 1956*
*International Aggregate Championship 1956*
*Scottish Aggregate Trophy 1956*

### Pedigree Details

|  |  |  |
|---|---|---|
| **SWEEP 3834, W. Hislop** | ┌GLEN 3510, W. J. Hislop | ┌BEN 1572, A. Ridell<br>└BEAT I, J. Guthrie |
|  | └NELL 3514, W. J. Hislop | ┌CAP 3036, J. M. Wilson<br>└MOSS 1827, J. McCaskie |
| **JED 3403, J. Swinton** | ┌JIGGS 2378, G. P. Brown | ┌BEN 1572, A. Ridell<br>└TIB I, J. Anderson |
|  | └FLY 2496, J. A. Hogg | ┌BOY, G. Dalgleish<br>└LASSIE III, J. Hogarth |

**SWEEP 3834**　*International Farmers' Champion 1946*
*Scottish National Champion & Driving Champion 1948*

# MOSS 11029

(R. Ackrill)

**Born 6/4/53   Black, mottled & white     J. H. Holliday, Pateley Bridge**

**Awards**

*International Aggregate Championship 1957*
*English Aggregate Championship 1957 & 1959*
*John H. Thorpe Memorial Trophy 1958*

**Pedigree Details**

| | | |
|---|---|---|
| ROY 5406, J. H. Holliday | ROGER 4323, J. H. Holliday | BEN 2851, J. Holmes<br>MEG 2848, J. H. Holliday |
| | KATE – , Harker | Not known<br>Not known |
| BESS 7936, M. Kay | MOSS 5176, J. M. Wilson | MIRK 4438, J. M. Wilson<br>NELL 3514, J. Kirk |
| | FLY 3592, J. Gilchrist | DRIFT 3453, W. Rutherford<br>QUEEN 3564, W. Rutherford |

**ROY 5406**   *English National Champion 1951*
            *English Driving Champion 1950*
**MOSS 5176**   *International Aggregate Championship 1949*
            *Scottish Aggregate Championship 1949 & 1951*
**MIRK 4438**   *International Supreme Champion 1950*
            *International & Scottish Aggregate Championships 1950*
            *Scottish National Champion 1950*

# TWEED 9601

**Born 9/10/52    Black, white & tan    W. J. Evans, Tidenham**

## Awards

*English National Champion 1959*
*English Driving Champion 1961*
*English Brace Champion with Moss 7971, 1958 & 1960*
*International Aggregate Championship 1958*
*English Aggregate Championship 1958*

## Pedigree Details

| | | |
|---|---|---|
| **MOSS 5176, J. M. Wilson** | ┌MIRK 4438, J. M. Wilson | ┌SPOT 3369, J. McDonald<br>└CHRIS 4065, J. Cole |
| | └NELL 3514, J. Kirk | ┌CAP 3036, J. M. Wilson<br>└MOSS 1827, McCaskie |
| **TRIM 8859, R. Anderson** | ┌SPOT II 6775, W. R. Little | ┌GLEN 3957, S. Banks<br>└TIB 4458, S. Banks |
| | └PHIL 6132, W. R. Little | ┌MIRK 4438, J. M. Wilson<br>└QUEEN 4205, J. M. Wilson |

**MOSS 5176**    *International Aggregate Championship 1949*
*Scottish Aggregate Championship 1949 & 1951*
**MIRK 4438**    *International Supreme Champion 1950*
*International & Scottish Aggregate Championships 1950*
*Scottish National Champion 1950*
**SPOT II 6775**    *Scottish National Champion 1954*

# BEN 13879

(Sport & General Press Agency)

**Born 25/2/56    Black, white & mottled    M. Jones, Llandrillo**

**Awards**
*International Farmers' Champion 1959*
*International Aggregate Championship 1959*
*Welsh Aggregate Championship 1959*

## Pedigree Details

| JAFF 8228, H. Herbert | ⌈JAFF 4313, R. J. Hughes | ⌈COON 1608, Lord Mostyn<br>⌊NELL, T. O. Jones |
| | ⌊MONA 5017, T. H. Lewis | ⌈LADDIE 3135, Hughes<br>⌊MONA, Parry |
| MEG 11130, E. Jones | ⌈LAD 7348, J. H. Denniff | ⌈GLEN 3940, J. M. Wilson<br>⌊NAN 5540, B. Wilson |
| | ⌊FLY 5681, M. Denniff | ⌈MOSS, Williams<br>⌊QUEEN 4477, Williams |

JAFF 4313    *International & Welsh Driving Champion 1946, 1947 & 1949*
            *Welsh National Champion 1946 & 1948*
            *Welsh Brace Champion 1946*

GLEN 3940    *International Supreme Champion 1946 & 1948*
            *International Farmers' Champion 1948*
            *International & Scottish Aggregate Championships 1946 & 1948*
            *Scottish National Champion 1946*

## KEN 13306

(News Chronicle)

**Born 3/12/55    Black, white & tan    E. L. Daniel, Ystradgynlais**

### Awards

*Welsh Driving Champion 1959*
*Welsh Aggregate Championship 1960*

### Pedigree Details

| | | |
|---|---|---|
| **CHIP 4924, D. W. Daniel** | MOSS – , W. Elliott | Not known<br>Not known |
| | TIB – , D. Dickson | Not known<br>Not known |
| **FLOSS 11400, D. W. Daniel** | MOSS 7878, T. Bonella | MOSS 3831, J. McKershar<br>SWAN, D. Cowan |
| | MOSS 5922, W. Wardrop | MIRK 4438, J. M. Wilson<br>QUEEN 3389, T. Bonella |

**CHIP 4924**  *International Supreme Champion 1949 & 1952*
**FLOSS 11400**  *Welsh Aggregate Championship 1955 & 1957*
**MOSS 7878**  *Scottish National Champion 1956*
**MIRK 4438**  *International Supreme Champion 1950*
*International & Scottish Aggregate Championships 1950*
*Scottish National Champion 1950*

## ROY 15393

(Daily Express)

**Born 4/4/57    Black, white & tan    A. Jones, Pontllyfni**

### Awards

*International Farmers' Champion 1961*
*International Brace Champion with Glen 17251, 1964*
*Welsh National Champion 1959 & 1961*
*Welsh Farmers' Champion 1961*
*Welsh Driving Champion 1961*
*Welsh Brace Champion with Spot 9476, 1961*
*Welsh Brace Champion with Glen 17251, 1962 & 1964*
*International Aggregate Championship 1961*
*Welsh Aggregate Championship 1961*
*The Challis Shield 1959 & 1961*
*Brace Aggregate Trophy with Glen 17251, 1964*

## Pedigree Details

| | | |
|---|---|---|
| **ROY 7696,** W. J. Evans | MAC 5498, J. Evans | JAFF 4313, R. J. Hughes<br>MINN 3387, J. C. Williams |
| | MEG 6782, G. W. Jones | GLEN 2584, J. Jones<br>MON 3417, T. Jones |
| **JILL 7742,** W. J. Evans | MOSS 5176, J. M. Wilson | MIRK 4438, J. M. Wilson<br>NELL 3514, J. Kirk |
| | NELL 6879, W. J. Evans | MOSS 6811, A. Jones<br>FLY N.R., R. Wood |

**ROY 7696**   *International Supreme Champion 1953*

**MOSS 5176**   *International Aggregate Championship 1949*
         *Scottish Aggregate Championship 1949 & 1951*

**NELL 6879**   *Welsh Aggregate Championship 1951*
         *International Farmers' Champion 1953*
         *Brace Aggregate Championship 1956*
         *Welsh Brace Champion 1951, 1953 & 1956*

**JAFF 4313**   *International & Welsh Driving Champion 1946, 1947 & 1949*
         *Welsh National Champion 1946 & 1948*
         *Welsh Brace Champion 1946*

**MINN 3387**   *Challis Shield*

**MIRK 4438**   *International Supreme Champion 1950*
         *International & Scottish Aggregate Championships 1950*
         *Scottish National Champion 1950*

**MOSS 6811**   *International Aggregate Championship 1952*
         *Welsh Aggregate Championship 1950 & 1952*
         *Welsh Brace Champion 1952*

*A. Jones with Roy*                    (Daily Express)

# GARRY 17690

**Born 10/2/60   Black & white   A. T. Lloyd, Builth Wells**

## Awards

*International Aggregate Championship 1962*
*Welsh Aggregate Championship 1962*
*Captain Whittaker Outwork Cup 1962*

## Pedigree Details

| | | |
|---|---|---|
| **GARRY 11742, H. Greenslade** | GLEN 7690, H. Greenslade | SWEEP 4204, W. J. Evans / JED 4047, W. James |
| | FLOSS 10217, C. Cook | JIM 9968, R. R. H. Griffiths / JET 9814, C. Cook |
| **NELL 16024, A. T. Lloyd** | CHIP 4924, D. W. Daniel | MOSS, W. Elliott / TIB, D. Dickson |
| | FLOSS 11400, D. W. Daniel | MOSS 7878, T. Bonella / MOSS 5922, W. Wardrop |

**GARRY 11742**   *Challis Shield 1963*

**GLEN 7690**   *International Farmers' Champion 1956*

               *Welsh National Champion 1955 & 1956*

               *Welsh Driving Champion 1956*

**CHIP 4924**   *International Supreme Champion 1949 & 1952*

**FLOSS 11400**   *Welsh Aggregate Championship 1955 & 1957*

**SWEEP 4204**   *Welsh National Champion 1949*

**JED 4047**   *Challis Shield 1955 & 1956*

**MOSS 7878**   *Scottish National Champion 1956*

# JUNO 17815

**Born 9/3/60    Black, white & tan    H. J. Worthington, Abergavenny**


### Awards
*Welsh National Champion 1967*
*Welsh Farmers' Champion 1967*
*Welsh Driving Champion 1964 & 1965*
*Welsh Aggregate Championship 1963*
*International Aggregate Championship 1963*

| | | |
|---|---|---|
| | ┌ROY 7696, W. J. Evans | ┌MAC 5498, J. Evans<br>└MEG 6782, G. Jones |
| HEMP 13132, H. J. Worthington | └FLOSS 8582, H. J. Worthington | ┌LAD 6393, J. R. Millar<br>└BESS 6547, A. Lambie |
| | ┌MOSS 4975, H. J. Worthington | ┌BEN 2812, J. Holmes<br>└MEG 4449, J. Holmes |
| FLY 12570, H. J. Worthington | └FLOSS 8582, H. J. Worthington | ┌LAD 6393, J. R. Millar<br>└BESS 6547, A. Lambie |

**HEMP 13132**  *International Brace Champion 1960 & 1961*
*Welsh Shepherds' Champion & Brace Champion 1959*
*Brace Aggregate Championship 1960 & 1961*

**FLY 12570**  *International Shepherds' Champion 1959*
*International Brace Champion & Aggregate Championship*
*1960 & 1961*
*Welsh Shepherds' Aggregate Championship 1959*
*Welsh Brace Champion 1959*

**ROY 7696**  *International Supreme Champion 1953*

**MOSS 4975**  *International Shepherds' Champion 1951 & 1953*
*Welsh Shepherds' Champion 1949, 1951, 1953 & 1954*

# CRAIG 15445

**Born 19/4/57 Black & white L. R. Suter, Cross Keys**

### Awards
*Welsh Aggregate Cup 1964*
*Captain Whittaker Outwork Cup 1964*

### Pedigree Details

| | | |
|---|---|---|
| **GLEN 7690, H. Greenslade** | ┌SWEEP 4204, W. J. Evans | ┌GLEN 3940, J. M. Wilson<br>└JED, J. Purdie |
| | └JED 4047, W. James | ┌CAP 3036, J. M. Wilson<br>└JED 3565, T. Lothian |
| **FLOSS 10217, C. Cook** | ┌JIM 9968, R. R. H. Griffiths | ┌MOSS 5176, J. M. Wilson<br>└NELL 6879, W. J. Evans |
| | └JET 9814, C. Cook | ┌SWEEP 4204, W. J. Evans<br>└JED 4047, H. Greenslade |

**GLEN 7690**  *International Farmers' Champion 1956*
*Welsh National Champion 1955 & 1956*
*Welsh Driving Champion 1956*

**SWEEP 4204**  *Welsh National Champion 1949*

**GLEN 3940**  *International Supreme Champion 1946 & 1948*
*International Farmers' Champion 1948*
*International & Scottish Aggregate Championships 1946 & 1948*
*Scottish National Champion 1946*

**MOSS 5176**  *International Aggregate Championship 1949*
*Scottish Aggregate Championship 1949 & 1951*

**NELL 6879**  *International Farmers' Champion 1953*
*Welsh Aggregate Championship 1951*
*International Brace Aggregate Championship 1956*
*Welsh Brace Champion 1951, 1953 & 1956*

**JED 4047**  *Challis Shield 1955 & 1956*

# WISTON CAP 31154

**Born 28/9/63  Black, white & tan  J. Richardson, Peebles**

## Awards
*International Shepherds' Champion 1966*
*Scottish Driving Champion 1969*

## Pedigree Details

| | | |
|---|---|---|
| | ┌COON 10011, J. Richardson | ┌ GLEN 7313, J. Richardson<br>└ MEG 7509, R. Hunter |
| CAP 15839, J. Richardson | | |
| | └LYN 13707, R. Frame | ┌ KEN 10936, R. Hunter<br>└ FAY 11960, R. Frame |
| | ┌BILL II 17937, J. M. Wilson | ┌ WHITEHOPE NAP 8685, J. M. Wilson<br>└ MEG 12223, J. Howie |
| FLY 25005, W. S.<br>Hetherington | | |
| | └LASSIE 19421, J. Hogarth | ┌ WISTON BOBBY II 9904, W. S. Hetherington<br>└ PHIL 13063, J. Hogarth |

**WHITEHOPE NAP 8685**  *Scottish National Champion 1955*

WISTON CAP – magical words. Who in the world of shepherds and sheepdogs does not know of him? The most popular and used stud dog in the history of the breed. A handsome, biddable, good-natured, splendid hill dog; a genuine shepherding dog, trained and handled by John Richardson, and bred by W. S. Hetherington. He was a product of very clever blending of blood lines all tracing back to the early registered dogs of the stud book, and line bred to J. M. Wilson's Cap 3036, who occurs sixteen times within seven generations, in his pedigree.

Wiston Cap sired three Supreme Champions and is grand-sire of three others, one of these, E. W. Edwards' Bill, having won the accolade twice. Among the many trial champions bred from Wiston Cap the most renowned are John Richardson's Mirk 52844, Scottish National and Driving Champion in 1975, and Scottish Shepherds' Champion in 1973 and 1975. The black-coated Sweep 39603 was Scottish Shepherds' and Driving Champion in 1968.

Wiston Cap lived to be fifteen and a half years old; he became a legend in his own lifetime. The International Sheep Dog Society badge portrays him in characteristic pose. He is buried on the hillside where the peaceful bleating of sheep is the only sound to break the silence, where the first rays of the morning sun shine warm on his resting place. The charismatic Wiston Cap was only a sheepdog, but one whose name will be remembered for all time in the annals of Border Collie history.

## KEN 17166

(Evening Standard)

**Born 14/4/60    Black & white    Tim Longton, Quernmore**

### Awards

*International Farmers' Champion 1964*
*English National Champion 1966*
*English Farmers' Champion 1964 & 1966*
*English Aggregate Championship 1964 & 1966*
*Captain Whittaker Outwork Cup 1966*
*John H. Thorpe Memorial Trophy 1966*

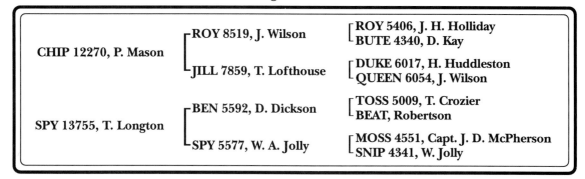

ROY 5406   *English National Champion 1951*
*English Driving Champion 1950*
MOSS 4551   *English Driving Champion 1947 & 1948*

ENGLAND'S most successful trial winning family is the Longtons from the Quernmore area of the Pennines.

In 1949, Tim Longton senior won the English Championship with Dot 4844, with whom he was reserve Supreme Champion in 1954 at Worcester. His six sons have all gained successes in trials, Will being English Shepherds' Champion 1957 with Roy 7729, and Jack has been a member of the English team on numerous occasions.

But it is Tot and Tim who are the renowned handlers. Tot has been competing for over forty years, winning two English National Championships with Mossie 6235, in 1950 and 1956, and nine English Brace Championships: with Bute 6236 and Mossie in 1954; Dot 4844 and Roy 7729 in 1955; Nell 12462 and Spot 13736 in 1959 and 1961; Nell 12462 and Mirk 16993 in 1962; Nip 16878 and Rob 21959 in 1968; Lad 41928 and Rob 21959 in 1969, when they were also International Brace Champions; and Lad 41928 and Gyp 38336 in 1971 and 1972.

In 1971 Gyp qualified to compete in all sections at the International. She was third in the qualifying trials, won the driving class, was fourth in the brace class and became reserve Supreme Champion to J. Murray's Glen, having run the Supreme Championship gathering course twice, because the first twenty sheep were found to be mismarked. As the culmination to his successes Tot Longton won the 1983 Supreme Championship with Jess, who had been second that year in the English National.

Tim Longton was English Shepherds' Champion in 1951 with Nell 7077, while employed as shepherd for the Water Board, and proceeded in the coming years to win the English National Championship five times – with Snip 16879 in 1965, Ken 17166 in 1966, Glen II 48637 in 1970, Roy 54175 in 1974 and Tweed 96630 in 1981. Snip, Glen II, Roy and Tweed each won the English Farmers' Championship, with Ken winning the title on two occasions. Ken and Tweed were also International Farmers' Champions in 1964 and 1980 respectively. Ken became Supreme Champion at Chester in 1966, and 1973, 1974 and 1975 saw Roy 54175 and Cap 67711 winning the English Brace Championship, which Tim won again in 1978 with Bess 89022 and Tweed.

Tot Longton's son Thomas is successfully emulating his father – he won the English National and Farmers' Championships in 1985 with Bess 101142, who partnered Lassie 91601 in 1979 and 1982, Maggie 140478 in 1985 and her daughter Gem 147666 in 1987 to win four English Brace Championships. Tweed 140476, a full brother to Maggie, won the 1987 English Driving Championship. Bess crowned her trials career with the Supreme Championship in 1986.

Tim Longton's son Timothy won the 1988 English Brace Championship at his first attempt, with Gel 124181 and Cap 161769, while twenty-year-old Brian Dodd, Tim's grandson, won the English National Championship with Laddie 151099, a son of his grandfather's old red Tweed.

It is noteworthy that the Longton family is still continuing their successes: Tim Longton won the 1993 English Brace Championship with Glen 165274 and Becca 170072 and has been a team member with both dogs. His son Timothy won the 1990 English Brace Championship with Gel 124181 and Cap 161769, while Tot Longton's son, Thomas, won the 1992 English National with Gem 147666, who was also Driving Champion. Gem, in partnership with Tweed 140476, won the English Brace Championships in 1989 and 1991, Tweed also being English Driving Champion in 1991. Thomas Longton again won the English Brace Championship in 1994 with Pam 182214 and Fern 190271.

Residing in the same area and relatives of the Longtons are the Huddleston family, members of which have been successful trial competitors for many years, and they have, like so many families, bred their working dogs from the same strain through their long association with the sheepdog. Harry Huddleston from Carnforth, who has competed in trials for over fifty years, won the Supreme Championship with Bett in 1969 and the 1989 English National with Jim 150661. The 'other' Harry Huddleston, breeding from the same long line of proven dogs, owned Udale Sim 52690, winner in 1972 of the English National, English Farmers' and the English Aggregate Championships.

Udale Sim competed in the 1973 New Zealand Expo World Championship trials and returned to Britain with Harry. When nine years old, Sim was sold to return to New Zealand for stud purposes, but sadly died during the flight. A bitch sired by him while he was in New Zealand in 1973 became a renowned and successful trial dog.

A further relative of these two families, J. K. Gorst, has also been a successful trials competitor, breeding from the same 'family' of dogs, which has often produced the seldom seen slate-blue coat colour. Joe Gorst won the English National and International Driving Championships in 1953 with Bet 6260, who in 1953 and 1954 also won the English Driving Championships. Queen 8810 also won the English National Championship in 1957 and was reserve National Champion to W. J. Evans' Tweed in 1959. Bet 6260 was grandam of Harry Huddleston's 1969 Supreme Champion, Bett.

# GAEL 14463

**Born 6/4/57     Black & white     T. T. McKnight, Canonbie**

### Awards

*International Brace Champion with Dot III 18925, 1967*
*Scottish National Champion 1964*
*Scottish Farmers' Champion 1964*
*Scottish Driving Champion 1967*
*Scottish Brace Champion with Dot III 18925, 1965, 1966 & 1967*
*International Aggregate Championship 1965 & 1967*
*Scottish Aggregate Trophy 1965 & 1967*
*Brace Aggregate Trophy with Dot III 18925, 1967*
*Captain Whittaker Outwork Cup 1967*

## Pedigree Details

| | | |
|---|---|---|
| **WHITEHOPE NAP 8685,** J. M. Wilson | ┌ GLEN 6123, W. McClure | ┌ MARK 4991, J. Jones<br>└ FLOSS 5058, J. Jones |
| | └ MEG 5141, W. McClure | ┌ JIM N. R., Scott<br>└ NELL 3514, J. Kirk |
| **DOT 11228, T. T. McKnight** | ┌ JIM 5856, R. Swan | ┌ DRIFT 4380, J. R. Millar<br>└ MEG 5623, D. Young |
| | └ TIB 5881, D. Young | ┌ MOSS 4551, Capt. J. McPherson<br>└ JED 4770, D. Young |

**WHITEHOPE NAP 8685**   *Scottish National Champion 1955*
**DRIFT 4380**   *Scottish Driving Champion 1946*
**MOSS 4551**   *English Driving Champion 1947 & 1948*

# BOSWORTH COON 34186

(E. B. Carpenter)

**Born 16/4/64    Black, white & mottled    L. Evans, Towcester**

### Awards
*International Farmers' Champion 1969*
*English National Champion 1969*
*English Farmers' Champion 1969*
*International Aggregate Championship 1969*
*English Aggregate Championship 1968 & 1969*
*Captain Whittaker Outwork Cup 1968*
*John H. Thorpe Memorial Trophy 1969*

```
BOSWORTH SCOT 22120,        ┌BEN 13864, R. MacKay       ┌WHITEHOPE NAP 8685, J. M. Wilson
           L. Evans         │                           └TIBBY 6582, R. MacKay
                            │
                            └LASS 11713, D. Dickson     ┌BEN 5592, D. Dickson
                                                        └NELL 5426, D.Dickson

                            ┌HAIG 9190, T. Jones        ┌SPEED 4382, J. R. Millar
FLY 13724, L. Evans         │                           └FLY 9168, J. Duncan
                            │
                            └FLY 9731, R. Davies        ┌PATCH 6531, T. Roberts
                                                        └JUNO 4869, R. Davies
```

**BOSWORTH SCOT 22120**   *International Driving Champion 1962*

**HAIG 9190**   *Welsh Driving Champion 1960*

**WHITEHOPE NAP 8685**   *Scottish National Champion 1955*

**SPEED 4382**   *Scottish Aggregate Championship 1952*

**JUNO 4869**   *Challis Shield 1957*

97

# BETT 40428

**Born 10/2/63    Black & white    H. Huddleston, Carnforth**

### Awards

*Captain Whittaker Outwork Cup 1969*
*R. Fortune Trophy 1969*
*John H. Thorpe Memorial Trophy 1967*

### Pedigree Details

| | | |
|---|---|---|
| ROY 14152, J. Gorst | ROY 8961, E. Holliday | ROY 5406, J. H. Holliday<br>BUTE 4340, D. Kay |
| | BET 6260, J. Gorst | SHEP 6107, J. K. Gorst<br>MADDIE 4337, H. Huddleston |
| Unnamed dam, N.R. | Not known | Not known<br>Not known |
| | Not known | Not known<br>Not known |

**BET 6260** *English National Champion & International Driving Champion 1953*

*English Driving Champion 1953 & 1954*

*John H. Thorpe Memorial Trophy 1953*

**ROY 5406** *English National Champion 1951*

*English Driving Champion 1950*

# WISTON BILL 36391

(International Sheep Dog Society)

**Born 29/10/64   Black, white & tan    D. McTeir, Peebles**

### Awards
*International Aggregate Championship 1970*
*Scottish Aggregate Trophy 1970*
*Captain Whittaker Outwork Cup 1970*
*R. Fortune Trophy 1970*

## Pedigree Details

| | | |
|---|---|---|
| **MIRK 13296, D. McTeir** | GLEN 12063, D. Murray | NUMBER 6152, D. Murray |
| | | QUEEN 7439, W. McMorran |
| | QUEEN 10906, R. Fortune | COON 8042, D. MacLeod |
| | | FLOSS 4603, J. Morrison |
| **FLY 25005, W. S. Hetherington** | BILL II 17937, J. M. Wilson | WHITEHOPE NAP 8685, J. M. Wilson |
| | | MEG 12223, J. Howie |
| | LASSIE 19421, J. Hogarth | WISTON BOBBY II 9904, W. S. Hetherington |
| | | PHIL 13063, J. Hogarth |

**MIRK 13296**   *International Shepherds' Champion 1964*
*International & Scottish Driving Champion 1964*
*International & Scottish Aggregate Championships 1964*
*Scottish Shepherds' Aggregate Championship 1964 & 1965*

**GLEN 12063**   *International Driving Champion 1960*
*Scottish Driving Champion 1960*

**NUMBER 6152**   *International Brace Champion 1953, 1954 & 1955*
*Brace Aggregate Championship 1951, 1953, 1955*
*Scottish Brace Champion 1951, 1952, 1953 & 1954*

**WHITEHOPE NAP 8685**   *Scottish National Champion 1955*

# GLEN 47241

(T. Phin)

**Born 18/4/67**     **Black, white & mottled**     **J. Murray, Sanquhar**

## Awards

*International Aggregate Championship 1971*
*Scottish Aggregate Trophy 1971*
*R. Fortune Trophy 1971*

### Pedigree Details

| | | |
|---|---|---|
| **WISTON CAP 31154,**<br>**J. Richardson** | ⌐CAP 15839, J. Richardson | ⌐COON 10011, J. Richardson<br>└LYN 13707, R. Frame |
| | └FLY 25005, W. S. Hetherington | ⌐BILL II 17937, J. M. Wilson<br>└LASSIE 19421, J. Hogarth |
| **KATEY 20820, J. Murray** | ⌐LAD 12476, J. Sharp | ⌐LAD 4276, A. G. Hyslop<br>└BET 10810, W. Kelly |
| | └GUESS 12754, J. T. M. Thompson | ⌐JIM 5856, Swan<br>└FLO 5038, J. T. M. Thompson |

WISTON CAP 31154     *International Supreme Champion 1965*

(Scottish Farmer)

**Born 25/10/67   Black & white   J. J. Templeton, Kilmarnock**

### Awards

*International Brace Champion with Fleet 37588, 1972*
*Scottish Farmers' Champion 1972*
*Scottish Brace Champion with Fleet 37588, 1972*
*International Aggregate Championship 1972*
*Brace Aggregate Trophy with Fleet 37588, 1972*
*Scottish Aggregate Trophy 1972*
*Captain Whittaker Outwork Cup 1972*
*R. Fortune Trophy 1972*

WISTON CAP 31154, J. Richardson
- CAP 15839, J. Richardson
  - COON 10011, J. Richardson
  - LYN 13707, R. Frame
- FLY 25005, W. S. Hetherington
  - BILL II 17937, J. M. Wilson
  - LASSIE 19421, J. Hogarth

MOIRA 19110, R. Carr
- ROY 12780, W. Corbett
  - KEN 10879, C. Cumming
  - FLOSS 10157, C. Cumming
- MEG 11600, G. Aitken
  - BEN 8144, R. Armstrong
  - BET 10521, D. Armstrong

**WISTON CAP 31154**   *International Supreme Champion 1965*

**Born 29/7/70    Black & white    H. G. Jones, Bodfari**

### Awards

*Welsh Brace Champion with Bwlch Bracken 74660, 1974*
*International Aggregate Championship 1973*
*Welsh Aggregate Cup 1973 & 1975*
*Captain Whittaker Outwork Cup 1973*
*R. Fortune Trophy 1973*
*Feedmobile Challenge Cup 1975*
*Lord Mostyn Plate 1973*
*ISDS Blue Riband 1973*
*Pedigree Chum Supreme Championship Trophy 1973*

## Pedigree Details

| | | |
|---|---|---|
| **CRAIG 47577, E. Griffith** | SPOT 24981, J. Gilchrist | BOB 12684, J. Gilchrist<br>WISTON NAN III 9896, P.McG. Hepburn |
| | MIST 39205, J. Bathgate | ROCK 27425, J. Bathgate<br>BUNT 20762, J. Cole |
| **NELL 43755,<br>W. T. Williams** | ROBIN 26091, E. Griffith | SHEP 18504, T. Watson<br>LASS 11655, J. Wood |
| | QUEEN 37247, D. Evans | CRAIG 23995, W. King<br>TESS 18268, W. King |

**SPOT 24981**    *International Aggregate, Scottish Aggregate & Scottish Shepherds' Aggregate Championships 1966*
*Scottish National Champion & Scottish Shepherds' Champion 1965 & 1966*

# BILL 51654

**Born 5/2/68    Black & white     G. Jones, Penmachno**

### Awards

*International Driving Champion 1974*
*Welsh Driving Champion 1974*
*International Aggregate Championship 1974*
*Welsh Aggregate Cup 1974*
*Captain Whittaker Outwork Cup 1974*
*R. Fortune Trophy 1974*
*Lord Mostyn Plate 1974*
*ISDS Blue Riband 1974*
*Pedigree Chum Supreme Champion Trophy 1974*

| | | |
|---|---|---|
| **WISTON CAP 31154,** J. Richardson | CAP 15839, J. Richardson | COON 10011, J. Richardson<br>LYN 13707, R. Frame |
| | FLY 25005, W. S. Hetherington | BILL II 17937, J. M. Wilson<br>LASSIE 19421, J. Hogarth |
| NAN 21068, W. Kinstrey | VIC II 12175, D. Murray | VIC 4368, D. Murray<br>JEN 11334, G. Robertson |
| | MAID 14667, D. H. Murray | GLEN 12063, D. Murray<br>JUNE 8216, D. Murray |

**WISTON CAP 31154**  *International Supreme Champion 1965*

**VIC 4368**  *International Brace Champion 1953, 1954 & 1955*
*Brace Aggregate Championship 1951, 1953 & 1955*
*International Driving Champion 1951*
*Scottish Brace Champion 1947, 1951, 1952, 1953 & 1954*
*Scottish National Champion 1952*
*Scottish Driving Champion 1950, 1951 & 1952*

**GLEN 12063**  *International & Scottish Driving Champion 1960*

# ZAC 66166

(C. A. Visual)

**Born 21/11/70   Black & white      R. C. MacPherson, MBE,
Brampton**

### Awards
*English Driving Champion 1975*
*International Aggregate Championship 1979*
*English Aggregate Championship 1975 & 1979*
*Captain Whittaker Outwork Cup 1979*
*R. Fortune Trophy 1975 & 1979*
*Lord Mostyn Plate 1975 & 1979*
*ISDS Blue Riband 1975 & 1979*
*Pedigree Chum Supreme Championship Trophy 1975 & 1979*
*Ivy Parry Trophy 1975*

## Pedigree Details

| | | |
|---|---|---|
| **KEN 47143, F. Coward** | ROB 21959, T. Longton | BOB 12684, J. Gilchrist<br>MINDRUM NELL 11106, R. S. Fraser |
| | MOSS 38505, J. Hadwin | MAC 28179, T. Wilson<br>MEG 28964, W. Swire |
| **QUEN 56602, J. Hadwin** | BOSWORTH COON 34186, L. Evans | BOSWORTH SCOT 22120, L. Evans<br>FLY 13724, L. Evans |
| | GYP 38336, T. Longton | BILL II 17937, J. M. Wilson<br>GYP 18044, D. Bevan |

**ROB 21959**   *International Brace Aggregate Champion 1969*
*English Brace Champion 1968 & 1969*

**BOSWORTH COON 34186**   *International Supreme Champion 1968*

**GYP 38336**   *International & English Driving Champion 1971*
*English Aggregate Championship 1971*
*English Brace Champion 1971 & 1972*

**MINDRUM NELL 11106**   *English Shepherds' Champion 1955*

**BOSWORTH SCOT 22120**   *International Driving Champion 1962*

# SHEP 73360

**Born 11/3/72    Black & white    G. Jones, Penmachno**

### Awards

*R. Fortune Trophy 1976*
*Lord Mostyn Plate 1976*
*ISDS Blue Riband 1976*
*Pedigree Chum Supreme Championship Trophy 1976*

### Pedigree Details

| | | |
|---|---|---|
| **SHEP II 49061,** S. H. Thomas | ┌WISTON CAP 31154, J. Richardson | ┌CAP 15839, J. Richardson<br>└FLY 25005, W. S. Hetherington |
| | └KIM 39897, J. Irving | ┌DON 18421, A. Livingstone<br>└MEG 15602, A. Ainslie |
| **TAMSIN 66472,** S. H. Thomas | ┌REX 58295, S. H. Thomas | ┌SPOT 45106, J. Laity<br>└JILL 46568, J. Laity |
| | └QUEEN 41968, S. H. Thomas | ┌ROY 21287, A. Jones<br>└MEG 27560, G. A. Lewis |

**WISTON CAP 31154**   *International Supreme Champion 1965*

# CRAIG 59425

**Born 18/12/69    Black & white    J. R. Thomas, Llandovery**

### Awards

*International Shepherds' Champion 1976 & 1977*
*Welsh National Champion 1977*
*Welsh Shepherds' Champion 1976 & 1977*
*International Aggregate Championship 1976 & 1977*
*Welsh Aggregate Trophy 1976 & 1977*
*Welsh Shepherds' Aggregate Trophy 1973, 1975, 1976 & 1977*
*Captain Whittaker Outwork Cup 1977*
*R. Fortune Trophy 1977*
*Lord Mostyn Plate 1977*
*ISDS Blue Riband 1977*
*Pedigree Chum Supreme Championship Trophy 1977*
*Challis Shield 1977*

## Pedigree Details

CHIP 29946, L. Suter
- BILL 16633, D. L. Evans
  - MOSS 4975, H. Worthington
  - FLOSS 8582, H. Worthington
- MEG 19713, R. H. Williams
  - ROY 14402, J. M. Baker
  - MEG 16167, J. M. Baker

JILL 49652, H. Hawken
- GARRY 19382, A. Chapman
  - CAP 7594, J. Walker
  - NELL 15388, J. Kirk
- JESS 37142, H. Hawken
  - CHIP 29946, L. Suter
  - NELL 23235, H. Hawken

**MOSS 4975** *International Shepherds' Champion 1951 & 1953*
*Welsh Shepherds' Aggregate Championship 1953 & 1954*
*Welsh Shepherds' Champion 1949, 1951, 1953 & 1954*

## MIRK 67512

**Born 23/1/71    Black, white &**     **R. J. Shennan, Turnberry**
**mottled**

### Awards

*International Driving Champion 1979*
*Scottish National Champion 1979*
*Scottish Farmers' Champion 1979*
*Scottish Driving Champion 1979*
*International Aggregate Championship 1978*
*Scottish Aggregate Trophy 1978*
*Captain Whittaker Outwork Cup 1978*
*R. Fortune Trophy 1978*
*Lord Mostyn Plate 1978*
*ISDS Blue Riband 1978*
*Pedigree Chum Supreme Championship Trophy 1978*
*Warnock Trophy 1978*
*Alexander Andrew Trophy 1979*
*J. M. Wilson Challenge Shield 1979*

## Pedigree Details

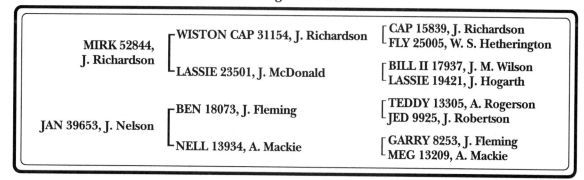

|  |  |  |
|---|---|---|
| **MIRK 52844,** J. Richardson | ┌ WISTON CAP 31154, J. Richardson | ┌ CAP 15839, J. Richardson └ FLY 25005, W. S. Hetherington |
|  | └ LASSIE 23501, J. McDonald | ┌ BILL II 17937, J. M. Wilson └ LASSIE 19421, J. Hogarth |
| **JAN 39653,** J. Nelson | ┌ BEN 18073, J. Fleming | ┌ TEDDY 13305, A. Rogerson └ JED 9925, J. Robertson |
|  | └ NELL 13934, A. Mackie | ┌ GARRY 8253, J. Fleming └ MEG 13209, A. Mackie |

**MIRK 52844**  *International Shepherds' Champion & Scottish Shepherds'*
*Aggregate Championship 1975*
*Scottish National Champion & Driving Champion 1975*
*Scottish Shepherds' Champion 1973 & 1975*
*Alexander Andrew Trophy 1975*
*J. M. Wilson Challenge Shield 1975*

**WISTON CAP 31154**  *International Supreme Champion 1965*

Two Scottish brothers have been successful in sheepdog trials. Robert Shennan won the Supreme Championship in 1978 with Mirk, who the following year won the Scottish National, Scottish Farmers', Scottish and International Driving Championships. In 1978 Mirk won the International and Scottish Aggregate Championships.

David Shennan won the 1976 and 1978 Scottish National Championships with Meg 63230 and Nan 85606 respectively. Meg won the Scottish Farmers' Championship in 1974 and 1976, and Nan won the Scottish Farmers'

and Driving Championships in 1978. Meg also won the Scottish Aggregate Championship in 1975. In 1963 with Roy 14746, David was International Farmers' Champion, as he was in 1971 with Maid 51269, who also won the Scottish Aggregate Championship in 1969. He also won this award in 1976 with Fly 73340.

Robert Shennan's seventeen-year-old son Jim was reserve in the Farmers' Championship with Tess at the 1975 Scottish National, joining his father and uncle in the Scottish team.

# ZAC 66166

(R. Fawcett)

**Born 21/11/70   Black & white   R. C. MacPherson, MBE
Brampton**

### Awards

*English Driving Champion 1975*
*International Aggregate Championship 1979*
*English Aggregate Championship 1975 & 1979*
*Captain Whittaker Outwork Cup 1979*
*R. Fortune Trophy 1975 & 1979*
*Lord Mostyn Plate 1975 & 1979*
*ISDS Blue Riband 1975 & 1979*
*Pedigree Chum Supreme Championship Cup 1975 & 1979*
*Ivy Parry Trophy 1975*

## Pedigree Details

```
                              ┌─ROB 21959, T. Longton           ┌ BOB 12684, J. Gilchrist
                              │                                 └ MINDRUM NELL 11106, R. S. Fraser
     KEN 47143, F. Coward     │
                              │                                 ┌ MAC 28179, T. Wilson
                              └─MOSS 38505, J. Hadwin           └ MEG 28964, W. Swire


                              ┌─BOSWORTH COON 34186, L. Evans   ┌ BOSWORTH SCOT 22120, L. Evans
                              │                                 └ FLY 13724, L. Evans
     QUEN 56602, J. Hadwin    │
                              │                                 ┌ BILL II, 17937, J. M. Wilson
                              └─GYP 38336, T. Longton           └ GYP 18044, D. Bevan
```

**ROB 21959**   *International Brace Champion 1969*
              *Brace Aggregate Championship 1969*
              *English Brace Champion 1968 & 1969*

**BOSWORTH COON 34186**   *International Supreme Champion 1968*

**GYP 38336**   *International & English Driving Champion 1971*
              *English Aggregate Championship 1971*
              *English Brace Champion 1971 & 1972*

**MINDRUM NELL 11106**   *English Shepherds' Champion 1955*

**BOSWORTH SCOT 22120**   *International Driving Champion 1962*

117

**JEN 93965**

(J. Fraser)

**Born 18/10/75   Black & white    T. Watson, Lauder**

## Awards

*International Shepherds' Champion 1978*
*Scottish Aggregate Trophy 1980*
*Scottish Shepherds' Aggregate Cup 1978 & 1980*
*Captain Whittaker Outwork Cup 1980*
*R. Fortune Trophy 1980*
*Lord Mostyn Plate 1980*
*ISDS Blue Riband 1980*
*Pedigree Chum Supreme Championship Trophy 1980*

## Pedigree Details

| | | |
|---|---|---|
| **ROY 74544, W. Jardine** | SWEEP 51651, R. Shennan | SWEEP 39603, J. Richardson<br>NELL 33597, I. Kerr |
| | MAID 51269, D. Shennan | TWEED 34916, J. Jack<br>FLY 44538, J. Jack |
| **NELL 61898, A. Munro** | SPOT 31731, D. Ross | STAR 13952, J. R. Millar<br>NELL 24986, R. Fleming |
| | NELL 37323, A. Munro | WISTON BEN III 9895, W. Hunter<br>NELL 20589, A. D. Cockburn |

**MAID 51269**  *International Farmers' Champion 1971*
*Scottish Aggregate Championship 1969*
**SWEEP 39603**  *International & Scottish Driving Champion 1968*
*Scottish Shepherds' Champion 1968*

**1981**                               **Armathwaite**

**1982**                               **Blair Atholl**

**BILL 78263**

(Marc Henrie)

**Born 4/1/73    Black & white    E. W. Edwards, Ruthin**

**Awards**

*International Farmers' Champion 1981*
*Welsh Farmers' Champion 1977*

*Welsh Driving Champion 1981*
*Welsh Brace Champion with Jaff 72449, 1979 & 1981*
*International Aggregate Championship 1981 & 1982*
*Brace Aggregate Trophy with Jaff 72449, 1981*
*Welsh Aggregate Cup 1981 & 1982*
*Captain Whittaker Outwork Cup 1981*
*R. Fortune Trophy 1981 & 1982*
*Lord Mostyn Plate 1981 & 1982*
*ISDS Blue Riband 1981 & 1982*
*Pedigree Chum Supreme Championship Trophy 1981 & 1982*
*Pedigree Chum Silver Salver 1981*

### Pedigree Details

| | | |
|---|---|---|
| **BILL 51654, G. Jones** | **WISTON CAP 31154, J. Richardson** | **CAP 15839, J. Richardson**<br>**FLY 25005, W. S. Hetherington** |
| | **NAN 21068, W. Kinstrey** | **VIC II 12175, D. Murray**<br>**MAID 14667, D. H. Murray** |
| **R. FLY 59282, Mrs M. K. Jones** | **FLEET 38813, J. Cropper** | **ROCK 27425, J. Bathgate**<br>**TRIM 26864, J. Bonella** |
| | **GAIL 42493, W. Robinson** | **BILL II 17937, J. M. Wilson**<br>**BET 25805, A. Gibson** |

**BILL 51654**  *International Supreme Champion 1974*
**WISTON CAP 31154**  *International Supreme Champion 1965*
**FLEET 38813**  *English Driving Champion 1968 & 1970*

(R. Fawcett)

(Marc Henrie)

**Born 9/10/74    Black & white    Tot Longton, Quernmore**

**Awards**

*International Aggregate Championship 1983*
*English Aggregate Championship 1983*
*Captain Whittaker Outwork Cup 1983*
*R. Fortune Trophy 1983*
*McDiarmid Trophy 1983*
*Lord Mostyn Plate 1983*
*ISDS Blue Riband 1983*

*Pedigree Chum Supreme Championship Trophy 1983*
*John H. Thorpe Memorial Trophy 1983*

## Pedigree Details

| KEN 77621, T. Longton | Not known | Not known |
| | | Not known |
| | NELL 25534, R. Singleton | VIC 10928, W. Sanderson |
| | | FLOSS 14878, R. Singleton |
| JILL 62096, W. Rockliffe | BOSWORTH COON 34186, L. Evans | BOSWORTH SCOT 22120, L. Evans |
| | | FLY 13724, L. Evans |
| | GYP 38336, T. Longton | BILL II, 17937, J. M. Wilson |
| | | GYP 18044, D. Bevan |

**BOSWORTH COON 34186** *International Supreme Champion 1968*

**GYP 38336** *International & English Driving Champion 1971*
*English Aggregate Championship 1971*
*English Brace Champion 1971 & 1972*

**BOSWORTH SCOT 22120** *International Driving Champion 1962*

(R. Fawcett)

# TURK 118169

(E. B. Carpenter)

**Born 7/12/79   Black & white   W. D. Reed, Upper Redbrook**

### Awards

*Welsh Aggregate Cup 1984*
*R. Fortune Trophy 1984*
*McDiarmid Trophy 1984*
*Lord Mostyn Plate 1984*
*ISDS Blue Riband 1984*
*Pedigree Chum Supreme Championship Trophy 1984*
*Rhiwlas Trophy 1984*

### Pedigree Details

|  |  |  |
|---|---|---|
| **JASPER 79280,** W. D. Reed | SWEEP 30913, W. D. Reed | GARRY 11742, H. Greenslade<br>NELL 16024, R. Brooks |
|  | FLY 67278, R. Barrel | CAP 59424, D. Williams<br>FLY 61950, D. Williams |
| **MEG 94933,** H. Lewis | NICK 41891, E. O. Jones | WHITEHOPE CORRIE 13706, J. McKee<br>BUTE 35077, J. McKee |
|  | MEG 57724, J. R. Saunders | ROY 46408, E. James<br>MEG 34297, T. C. Evans |

**JASPER 79280**   *International Driving Champion 1978*
**GARRY 11742**   *Challis Shield 1963*
**WHITEHOPE CORRIE 13706**   *Irish National Champion 1963*

## DON 122367

(Marc Henrie)

**Born 27/8/80    Black, white & tan     J. P. Mackenzie, Kinlochbervie**

### Awards

*Captain Whittaker Outwork Cup 1985*
*R. Fortune Trophy 1985*
*Lord Mostyn Plate 1985*
*ISDS Blue Riband 1985*
*Pedigree Chum Supreme Championship Trophy 1985*
*Rhiwlas Trophy 1985*

### Pedigree Details

|  |  |  |
|---|---|---|
| **MAC 115030, P. Ross** | ┌ **GLEN 79646, D. MacCuish** | ┌ **TWEED 65513, M. MacLeod**<br>└ **LASSIE 58841, M. MacLeod** |
|  | └ **MEG 72605, D. MacCuish** | ┌ **LAD 66684, A. Penrice**<br>└ **JILL 65828, D. Johnstone** |
| **GYP 93692, P. Ross** | ┌ **DON 38964, J. P. Mackenzie** | ┌ **HEMP 19886, W. Anderson**<br>└ **MONA 15834, S. Alexander** |
|  | └ **MEG 76329, P. Ross** | ┌ **BOB 50851, A. Lawrie**<br>└ **QUEEN 56809, N. MacLennon** |

(Marc Henrie)

**Born 19/12/76   Black, white & tan    T. W. Longton, Quernmore**

### Awards
*English National Champion 1985*
*English Farmers' Champion 1985*
*English Brace Champion with Lassie 91601, 1979 & 1982*
*English Brace Champion with Maggie 140478, 1985*
*English Brace Champion with Gem 147666, 1987*
*International Aggregate Championship 1986*

*English Aggregate Championship 1986*
*Captain Whittaker Outwork Cup 1986*
*R. Fortune Trophy 1986*
*Lord Mostyn Plate 1986*
*ISDS Blue Riband 1986*
*Pedigree Chum Supreme Championship Trophy 1986*
*Rhiwlas Trophy 1986*
*Langs' Scotch Whisky Quaiche 1986*
*John H. Thorpe Memorial Trophy 1985*
*Ivy Parry Trophy 1985*

## Pedigree Details

| | | |
|---|---|---|
| **GLEN 80138,** Mrs M. Arthurs | ┌ **MOSS 57707, A. Jones** | ┌ MOSS 41957, R. E. Nicholls └ NELL 39432, R. G. Evans |
| | └ **NELL 61154, A. Jones** | ┌ CRAIG 47577, E. Griffith └ FLY 49709, J. R. Griffith |
| **KERRY 84042,** T. Longton | ┌ **WISTON CAP 31154, J. Richardson** | ┌ CAP 15839, J. Richardson └ FLY 25005, W. S. Hetherington |
| | └ **GYP 56601, T. Longton** | ┌ BOSWORTH COON 34186, L. Evans └ GYP 38336, T. Longton |

**WISTON CAP 31154**  *International Supreme Champion 1965*
**MOSS 41957**  *Welsh National & Farmers' Champion 1972*
**BOSWORTH COON 34186**  *International Supreme Champion 1968*
*International Farmers' Champion 1969*
*English National & Farmers' Champion 1969*
*International Aggregate Championship 1969*
*English Aggregate Championship 1968 & 1969*
*Captain Whittaker Outwork Cup 1968*
*J. H. Thorpe Memorial Trophy 1969*
**GYP 38336**  *International & English Driving Champion 1971*
*English Aggregate Championship 1971*
*English Brace Champion 1971 & 1972*

# DAVY 131049

(Austin Bennett)

**Born 19/9/81    Black, white & tan     S. B. Price, Cressage**

### Awards
*English National Champion 1987*
*English Farmers' Champion 1987*
*English Aggregate Championship 1987*
*R. Fortune Trophy 1987*
*Lord Mostyn Plate 1987*
*ISDS Blue Riband 1987*
*Pedigree Chum Supreme Championship Trophy 1987*
*Rhiwlas Trophy 1987*
*Langs' Scotch Whisky Quaiche 1987*
*Sun Alliance Salver 1987*
*Ivy Parry Trophy 1987*

## Pedigree Details

| | | |
|---|---|---|
| **BOBBY 119815, T. Bowey** | ┌ **MOSS 91079, T. Bowey** | ┌ **DRIFT 68728, J. Bathgate**<br>└ **MEG 78015, J. Ironside** |
| | └ **SLIP 102578, T. Bowey** | ┌ **GLEN 75630, R. Fortune**<br>└ **NELL 53708, P. Hetherington** |
| **SANDIE 122755, J. Wilson** | ┌ **MAC 115688, J. Wilson** | ┌ **SWEEP 86362, W. Johnston**<br>└ **MAID 82040, J. McGregor** |
| | └ **VERA 93999, J. Wilson** | ┌ **GARRY 72142, D. Brown**<br>└ **FLY 81317, J. Gray** |

**GLEN 75630**  *Scottish Brace Champion 1977*
**NELL 53708**  *Scottish National & Shepherds' Champion 1970*
*Alexander Andrew Trophy 1970*

# SPOT 152290

(Austin Bennett)

**Born 12/8/82   Black, white & mottled      M. Jones, Ruthin**

### Awards
*International Farmers' Champion 1988*
*International Aggregate Championship 1988*
*Welsh Aggregate Championship 1988*
*Captain Whittaker Outwork Cup 1988*
*R. Fortune Trophy 1988*
*Lord Mostyn Plate 1988*
*ISDS Blue Riband 1988*
*Pedigree Chum Supreme Championship Trophy 1988*
*Rhiwlas Trophy 1988*
*Langs' Supreme Silver Quaiche 1988*
*Sun Alliance Silver Salver 1988*

## Pedigree Details

|  |  |  |
|---|---|---|
| **JAFF 128552,** D. Jones | ROB 81024, R. Clark | KEN 47143, F. Coward |
|  |  | QUEN 56602, J. G. Hadwin |
|  | GEMMA 92712, J. Taylor | KEN 86332, A. G. Heaton |
|  |  | NELL 67705, S. F. Mills |
| **DOVEY 127125,** H. M. Roberts | BEN 103519, S. Jones | MIRK 52844, G. Lloyd |
|  |  | JUNE 86004, T. J. Jones |
|  | BWLCH FLY 101364, H. M. Roberts | GLEN 92091, H. G. Jones |
|  |  | BWLCH BRACKEN 74660, Mrs B. Jones |

**MIRK 52844**    *International Shepherds' & Scottish Shepherds' Aggregate Championships 1975*
*Scottish National & Driving Champion 1975*
*Scottish Shepherds' Champion 1973 & 1975*
*Alexander Andrew Trophy 1975*
*J. M. Wilson Challenge Shield 1975*
**BWLCH BRACKEN 74660**    *Welsh Brace Champion 1974*

(Austin Bennett)

*Spot 152290 with the Blue Riband*

131

**WISP 161487**

(Austin Bennett)

**Born 24/2/86    Black & white    R. Dalziel, Ettrick Valley**

### Awards
*International Supreme Champion 1989 & 1992*
*ISDS Blue Riband 1989 & 1992*
*International Shepherds' Champion 1992*
*International Aggregate Championship 1989 & 1992*
*Scottish Aggregate Championship 1989*
*Lord Mostyn Plate 1989 & 1992*
*R. Fortune Trophy 1989 & 1992*
*Scottish Shepherds' Aggregate Championship 1992*
*Captain Whittaker Outwork Cup 1992*
*Pedigree Chum Supreme Champion Challenge Trophy 1989 & 1992*
*Lang's Supreme Silver Quaiche 1989 & 1992*
*Sun Alliance Group Crystal 1989*
*Caithness Glass 1992*
*Rhiwlas Trophy 1989 & 1992*
*Scottish National Champion 1992*

*Scottish Shepherds' Champion 1989, 1991 & 1992*
*Alexander Andrew Trophy 1991 & 1992*
*J.M. Wilson Challenge Shield 1992*

## Pedigree Details

| | | |
|---|---|---|
| **GUNNER KEELE 148409,** N. Rutter | **DON 108889, J. Thomas** | **CRAIG 59425, J. Thomas**<br>**MAID 97071, D. Jones** |
| | **FLY 114092, N. Rutter** | **ED 94619, R. Bailey**<br>**FLY 73214, R. Bailey** |
| **NELL 143510, J. Barr** | **BEN 119873, J. Templeton** | **GLEN 104763, J. Templeton**<br>**JEN 106069, J. Barr** |
| | **NELL 114326, J. Barr** | **MOSS 103923, J. Templeton**<br>**NELL 69129, J. Templeton** |

**DON 108889**  *English Aggregate Championship 1982*
*English Shepherds' Aggregate Championship 1982*
*English Shepherds' Champion 1984*

**BEN 119873**  *Scottish Brace Champion with Roy 114678, 1982, 1983 & 1984*
*International Brace Champion with ROY, 1984*
*Brace Aggregate Championship 1984*

**CRAIG 59425**  *International Supreme Champion 1977*
*International Shepherds' Champion 1976 & 1977*
*International Aggregate Championship 1976 & 1977*
*Welsh Aggregate Championship 1976 & 1977*
*Welsh Shepherds' Aggregate Championship 1973, 1975, 1976 & 1977*
*Captain Whittaker Outwork Cup 1977*
*R. Fortune Trophy 1977*
*Lord Mostyn Plate 1977*
*ISDS Blue Riband 1977*
*Pedigree Chum Supreme Championship Trophy 1977*
*Welsh National Champion 1977*
*Welsh Shepherds' Champion 1976 & 1977*
*Challis Shield 1977*

**MOSS 103923**  *Scottish Aggregate Championship 1979*
*Feedmobile Trophy 1979*

WISP 161487 is one of the very few dogs to have won the Supreme Championship twice. He first won in 1989 on the difficult Margam course, and repeated that triumph in 1992 on the long, flat Aberystwyth course. A spellbound audience watched his Supreme run at Aberystwyth: such rapport between man and dog is seldom witnessed and was recognised and appreciated by everyone that day.

He was also second in the Scottish National Championship in 1992, and in 1991 he was fifth in the Supreme Championship.

# QUEEN 152483

(Austin Bennett)

**Born 25/3/82    Black & white    G. Jones, Penmachno**

## Awards

*International Supreme Champion 1990*

*International Farmers' Champion 1990*

*Captain Whittaker Outwork Cup 1990, equal points with DON 141536*

*Lord Mostyn Plate 1990*

*R. Fortune Plate 1990*

*International Aggregate Championship 1990*

*Welsh Aggregate Championship 1990*

*ISDS Blue Riband 1990*

*Rhiwlas Cup 1990*

*Pedigree Chum Supreme Championship Trophy 1990*

*Pedigree Chum Silver Salver 1990*

*Welsh Driving Champion 1990*

*Welsh National Champion 1987*

*Welsh Farmers' Champion 1987*

*Challis Shield 1987*

*D.W. Davies Cup 1990*

| | | |
|---|---|---|
| **LAD 91117, J. M. Evans** | ┌ MOSS 72131, J. Millner | ┌ CRAIG 47577, E. Griffith<br>└ MEG 44766, T. J. Jones |
| | └ JUNNO 39329, J. M. Evans | ┌ NAP 29213, C. Lloyd<br>└ NELL 26622, J. M. Evans |
| **JILL 110568, R.O.M.,**<br>**M. Knight** | ┌ CRAIG 72737, A. Jones | ┌ MOSS 57707, A. Jones<br>└ NELL 61154, D. Owen |
| | └ BONNY 96510, C. Lloyd | ┌ VICK 74888, E. Griffith<br>└ FLOSS 74698, E. D. Morgan |

**CRAIG 72737**  *International Farmers' Champion 1977 & 1979*
*International Brace Champion 1980*
*International Driving Champion 1975 & 1976*
*Brace Aggregate Championship 1980*
*Feedmobile Challenge Cup 1977*
*McDiarmid Trophy 1976 & 1977*
*Pedigree Chum Silver Salver 1979*
*Welsh National & Welsh Farmers' Champion 1976*
*Welsh Driving Champion 1975, 1976 & 1977*
*Challis Shield 1976*

GWYN Jones is one of only three handlers to have won three Supreme Championships: in 1974 with Bill 51654, a son of Wiston Cap; in 1976 with Shep 73360, a grandson of Wiston Cap; and in 1990 with Queen, a grand-daughter of Alan Jones' Craig 72737.

Queen, who represented Wales on five occasions, was the Welsh National Champion in 1987, and was second in 1988 and 1990, when both titles were won by H. W. Jones' Meg 135659.

Bill 51654 was second in the 1974 Welsh National, and was in the 1976 Welsh team when his kennel mate, Shep, was Supreme Champion. Shep was a member of the Welsh team on four occasions. Bill sired E. W. Edwards' Bill 78263, who won the Supreme Championship in 1981 and 1982.

**1991**
**1994**

**SPOT 161819**

**Carmichael**
**Monymusk**

(Michael M. Trafford)

**Born 1/4/86    Black & white    J. H. Wilson, Ashkirk**

### Awards

*International Shepherds' Champion 1991 & 1994*
*International Aggregate Championship 1991*
*Scottish Shepherds' Aggregate Championship 1991*
*Scottish Aggregate Championship 1994*
*Feedmobile Trophy 1990*
*Lord Mostyn Plate 1991 & 1994*
*R. Fortune Trophy 1991 & 1994*
*ISDS Blue Riband 1991 & 1994*
*Rhiwlas Trophy 1991 & 1994*
*Pedigree Chum Supreme Championship Trophy 1991 & 1994*
*Caithness Glass 1991 & 1994*
*Warnock Trophy 1990*
*Allison Award 1991*

## Pedigree Details

```
                                                                    ┌ KEN II 18754, J. R. Millar
                              ┌ BEN 59446, D. W. Ross               └ MEG 17910, A. Penrice
        CAP 109820,           │
        R. C. MacPherson      │                                     ┌ MIRK 52844, J. Richardson
                              └ DRYDEN BUD 94291,                   └ DRYDEN QUEEN 70345, A. D. McGregor
                                J. Murdoch

                              ┌ CRAIG 113444, D. Baxter             ┌ CRAIG 59425, J. Thomas
                              │                                     └ MEG 87562, D. Baxter
        PEG 125220, J. H. Wilson
                              │                                     ┌ ROY 74544, W. Jardine
                              └ JEN 93965, T. Watson                └ NELL 61898, A. Munro
```

CAP 109820      *English Aggregate Championship 1981*
                *Feedmobile Trophy 1981*
PEG 125220      *International Shepherds' Champion 1984, 1986 and 1987*
                *International Aggregate Championship 1987*
                *Scottish Aggregate Championship 1986 & 1987*
                *Scottish Shepherds' Aggregate Championship 1986 & 1987*
                *Feedmobile Trophy 1986 & 1987*
                *Pedigree Chum Silver Salver 1986*
                *Scottish Shepherds' Champion 1987*
JEN 93965       *International Supreme Champion 1980*
                *International Shepherds' Champion 1978*
                *Scottish Aggregate Championship 1980*
                *Scottish Shepherds' Aggregate Championship 1978 & 1980*
                *Pedigree Chum Supreme Championship Trophy 1980*
                *Capt. Whittaker Outwork Cup 1980*
                *R. Fortune Trophy 1980*
                *Lord Mostyn Plate 1980*
                *ISDS Blue Riband 1980*
KEN II 18754    *Scottish National & Farmers' Champion 1969*
                *Alexander Andrew Trophy 1969*
MIRK 52844      *International Shepherds' Champion 1975*
                *Scottish Shepherds' Aggregate Championship 1973 & 1975*
                *Scottish National & Driving Champion 1975*
                *Scottish Shepherds' Champion 1973 & 1975*
                *Alexander Andrew Trophy 1975*
                *J. M. Wilson Challenge Shield 1975*
CRAIG 59425     *International Supreme Champion 1977*
                *International Shepherds' Champion 1976 & 1977*
                *International & Welsh Aggregate Championships 1976 & 1977*
                *Welsh Shepherds' Aggregate Championship 1973, 1975, 1976 & 1977*
                *Capt. Whittaker Outwork Cup 1977*

*R. Fortune Trophy 1977*

*Lord Mostyn Plate 1977*

*ISDS Blue Riband 1977*

*Pedigree Chum Supreme Championship Trophy 1977*

*Welsh National Champion 1977*

*Welsh Shepherds' Champion 1976 & 1977*

*Challis Shield 1977*

WINNING the Supreme Championship with Spot 161819 in 1991 and 1994 must have been especially gratifying to J. H. Wilson, as he had been in second place with Spot's dam, Peg 125220, in 1986 and 1987. Peg had also been third in 1989, and was the International Shepherds' Champion in 1984, 1986 and 1987, and Scottish Shepherds' Champion in 1987. Peg was a daughter of Tom Watson's Jen 93965, the 1980 Supreme Champion.

Spot, a son of R. C. MacPherson's Cap 109820, who was second in the 1981 Supreme Championship, was a member of the Scottish team in 1990 and 1992.

(Michael M. Trafford)

*J. H. Wilson with Spot and Peg*

(J. Mockford)

**Born 25/2/90    Black, white & tan    A. S. MacRae, Dollar**

### Awards

*International Farmers' Champion 1993 & 1994*
*International & Scottish Aggregate Championships 1993*
*Pedigree Chum Championship Trophy 1993*
*Pedigree Chum Silver Salver 1993 & 1994*
*Capt. Whittaker Outwork Cup 1993*
*Lord Mostyn Plate 1993*
*R. Fortune Trophy 1993*
*ISDS Blue Riband 1993*
*Rhiwlas Cup 1993*
*Caithness Glass 1994*

# Pedigree Details

| | | |
|---|---|---|
| **CRAIG 125319, K. Brehmer** | ⌈ MOSS 115753, J. McGowan | ⌈ GLEN 75630, R. Fortune<br>⌊ DOT 92152, T. Bell |
| | ⌊ JESSIE 101380, S. Jeffrey | ⌈ SHEP 67185, K. Shield<br>⌊ KIM 65808, W. Jackson |
| **FLY 131379, W. McAllister** | ⌈ MIRK 96612, J. A. Gordon | ⌈ SPOT 82060, G. Redpath<br>⌊ NELL 52793, G. Redpath |
| | ⌊ LYNN 101391, D. MacGregor | ⌈ MOSS 91079, C. Swan<br>⌊ JAN 81712, J. Walker |

**GLEN 75630**  *Scottish Brace Champion 1977*

(J. Mockford)

*A. S. MacRae with Nan 186565*

140

(J. Mockford)

**Born 22/2/90    Black & white    S. Davidson, Dunoon**

### Awards

*Scottish Aggregate Championship 1995*
*R. Fortune Trophy 1995*
*Lord Mostyn Plate 1995*
*ISDS Blue Riband 1995*
*Pedigree Chum Supreme Championship Trophy 1995*
*Rhiwlas Trophy 1995*

## Pedigree Details

| | | |
|---|---|---|
| **SCOT 110726, J. Paterson** | ┌BEN 53228, N. MacLean | ┌CRAIG 41757, J. Ramsay<br>└GAEL 46068, J. Ramsay |
| | └BESS 86506, Mrs E. Rogers | ┌GLEN 39063, I. McNaughton<br>└QUEEN 62173, J. Ramsay |
| **GELL 139418, J. Paterson** | ┌MOSS 103923, J. J. Templeton | ┌HEMP 72301, A. J. Campbell<br>└QUEEN 74047, H. MacKenzie |
| | └DOT 117976, D. Johnston | ┌BILL 102167, R. Fortune<br>└JAN 102280, J. Paterson |

**MOSS 103923**  *Scottish Aggregate Championship 1979*
*Feedmobile Challenge Cup 1979*
**HEMP 72301**  *Scottish Driving Champion 1977*

(Austin Bennett)

*S. L. Davidson with Craig 188525*

142

# Further Sources

## Books

Viv Billingham (1984), *One Woman and Her Dog*, Patrick Stephens Ltd.

E. B. Carpenter (1994), *National Sheepdog Champions of Britain and Ireland*, Farming Press Books.

Iris Combe (1978), *Border Collies*, Faber & Faber Ltd.

Iris Combe (1983), *Shepherds, Sheep and Sheepdogs*, Dalesman Books.

Sheila Grew (1981 & 1985), *Key Dogs from the Border Collie Family*, Vols. 1 and 2, Payne Essex Printers.

Sheila Grew (revised 1993), *Key Dogs from the Border Collie Family*, Vols. 1 and 2, Heritage Farms Publishing Company, U.S.A.

Eric Halsall (1980), *Sheepdogs, My Faithful Friends*, Patrick Stephens Ltd.

Eric Halsall (1982), *Sheepdog Trials*, Patrick Stephens Ltd.

John Holmes (1960), *The Farmer's Dog*, Popular Dogs Publishing Co. Ltd.

Tony Iley (1978), *Sheepdogs at Work*, Dalesman Books.

H. Glyn Jones & Barbara Collins (1987), *A Way of Life*, Farming Press Books.

R. B. Kelly (1942), *Sheepdogs*, Angus & Robertson, Australia.

Tim Longton & Edward Hart (1976), *The Sheepdog, Its Work and Training*, David and Charles.

J. H. McCulloch (1938), *Sheepdogs and Their Masters*, The Moray Press.

J. H. McCulloch (reprinted with additions 1994), *Sheepdogs and Their Masters*, Toft East Publishing, Lunenburg, MA, U.S.A.

J. H. McCulloch (1952), *Border Collie Studies*, The Pentland Press.

S. Moorehouse (1950), *The British Sheepdog*, H. F. & G. Witherby Ltd.

Matt Mundell (1981), *Country Diary*, Gordon Wright Publishing.

Marjorie Quarton (1986), *All About the Working Collie*, Pelham Books.

Peidje Vidler (1983), *The Border Collie in Australasia*, Gotrah Enterprises, Australia.

J. Wentworth-Day (1952), *The Wisest Dogs in the World*, Longshaw Sheepdog Trials Association.

## Magazines

*Working Sheepdog News* – bi-monthly, Delia Sturgeon, The Enterprise Centre, St Thomas Road, Launceston, Cornwall PL15 8BU.

*Outrun* – bi-monthly, Roy Goutté, Shepherds View, North Beer, Launceston, Cornwall PL15 8NP.

## Videos

Bruce Englefield, *Ewe Were Made for Me – Sheepdog Training for Beginners and Enthusiasts*. Bruce Englefield.

Glyn Jones, *Come Bye and Away!* Farming Press Videos.

Glyn Jones, *That'll Do!* Farming Press Videos.

Glyn Jones, *Take Time!* Farming Press Videos.

# DOG INDEX

*Index to champions, etc. and their occurrences in pedigrees; main references in bold.*

# GENERAL INDEX

*International Supreme Championship years are cited, followed by the page numbers in brackets. Other page numbers are general and family references.*